German
for Academic Purposes
An Introduction to Reading Academic Publications

German for Academic Purposes

An Introduction to Reading Academic Publications

By
Hanna Rogalla and Willy Rogalla

LANGENSCHEIDT

BERLIN · MUNICH · VIENNA · ZURICH · NEW YORK

Commissioned by the Goethe-Institut zur Pflege der deutschen Sprache im Ausland und zur Förderung der internationalen kulturellen Zusammenarbeit e.V.

Sponsored by the Stifterverband für die deutsche Wissenschaft e.V.

Translators: Frank H. Nelson and Peter Williams

Collaborators and Advisers: Heinrich Erk, Eduard Benes, Lore Armaleo-Popper, Albrecht Martiny

Criticism and Comments: Karin Herrmann, Claire Kristahn, Peter Green, Thomas Riepenhausen, Henk Siliakus, Rosemarie Buhlmann

Cover photo: Süddeutscher Verlag – Bilderdienst/G. Aczel

Course Material:

German for Academic Purposes
  An Introduction to Reading Academic Publications (49880)
Grammar Handbook for Reading German Texts (49881)

Printed in Germany · ISBN 3-468-49880-2

1 2 3 4 5 * 89 88 87 86 85

Introduction

Who is this book intended for?

This book is intended as an introduction for English-speaking readers who wish to be able to read in the original specialist journals and literature in the field of the humanities and the social sciences. It assumes some experience on the part of the user in the reading of non-fictional prose in English. Specialist subject knowledge and a knowledge of the German language are, however, not necessary.

It is intended to be used in a reading course. There should, however, on no account be more than 20 participants.

How much time is needed?

The book is designed to be worked through in sixty 45 minute sittings, assuming that the participants are prepared to go through the lessons again at home.

What is in the book?

The book is an introduction to the reading of German non-fictional prose. Its twenty-five chapters contain a selection of texts from book catalogues, publishers' advertising material, lectures and books. The texts are for the most part taken from the humanities and the social sciences. They are arranged in order of difficulty for the English-speaking reader.

In order to provide the reader with a framework within which he can orientate himself the texts are preceded by short references to the context from which they have been taken and to their source. There then follow exercises designed to improve the reader's comprehension of the text in step-by-step fashion and in more and more detail. Finally there are short descriptions of relevant points of grammar and word formation employing examples from the texts which precede.

More detailed descriptions of points of grammar and word formation can be found in the "Grammar Handbook"* to which the reader is referred.

The book is organized along contrastive lines. It is based on the lexical and structural similarities between the English and German languages as well as on the similarities in form and content in non-fictional prose.

In the first and second chapters English and German words of Germanic origin (cognates) are compared with one another and similarities and differences indicated.

In the second chapter a further common feature is emphasized, namely, the large number of common concepts of Latin and Greek origin (international words).

The texts contained in chapters 1 to 4 are book titles, headings, lists of contents and captions from illustrations. These text types contain a large number of noun phrases. In our experience it is profitable to first study these noun phrases in isolation, that is to say, outside of the framework of the sentence.

At the same time much basic vocabulary is presented in the first few chapters along with the most frequent function words in typical contexts. Some of the basic vocabulary also occurs in the form of illustrative derivations and combinations.

The first descriptive texts appear in chapters 5 to 8 and initially consist of one or two simple sentences. They contain a large number of verbal forms in the third person singular of the present tense – a characteristic of non-fictional prose.

Chapters 9 to 25 contain excerpts from various longer texts. Chapter 16 contains a continuation of the text in chapter 15. Chapter 17 is thematically related. The last three chapters 23 to 25 contain three passages from one text. These longer texts, which are spread over various chapters, exemplify, even if only in rudimentary fashion, the effectiveness of reading on. The reader becomes acquainted with a topic and on the basis of what he is already familiar with he can much more easily understand the passages which follow.

How do I work with this book?

Texts

The user should first read the references to the texts and sources in order to orientate himself.

The German text should be read aloud two or three times by the teacher in its entirety and at normal reading speed. If it is technically possible, the teacher should record each text on tape or cassette and make the recordings available to the students for homework purposes. While the teacher is reading the text aloud the students should follow the text silently in their books. If they can both hear and see the text at the same time, they can recognize through the intonation and accentuation the way the content of the text is structured and where the most essential information is concentrated.

The written form of new words and structures is much more easily committed to memory when supplemented by the spoken form.

Written Exercises

Each written exercise should first be attempted by the participants without any aid from the teacher – alone, in pairs or in groups. Finally the solutions should be discussed. Any difficulties which may have arisen should be explained. Only then should the next exercise be attempted.

In exercises where the text has to be quoted it is a good idea to write the solutions, once they have been suggested, on the blackboard or on a transparency for the overhead projector so that they can be discussed in forum. In the course of the discussion the quotations and the suggested English equivalents should be critically compared with one another in order to arrive at a perfect understanding of the relevant passages.

Basic forms from the dictionary or individual expressions and short sentences from the text should be written in German and only in the form in which they are to be found in the book, that is to say, they should be written down as literal quotations.

Writing down the examples also helps the participants to commit them to memory.

Oral Exercises

Exercises which are designed to be done orally should also first be discussed by the course participants who should, as far as is possible, try to find the correct solutions to them. The teacher should only intercede where no satisfactory solutions are forthcoming or in the event of the discussion moving too far away from the topic under discussion.

The participants are not required to speak German. They will, however, have to quote directly from the German text – only occasionally at the beginning but increasingly from chapter 7 onwards. The participants' pronunciation need only be intelligible – correctness is not the main priority at this stage.

The reading aloud of individual expressions or parts of speech is also a help in committing them to memory.

---

* Hanna Rogalla, Willy Rogalla: *Grammar Handbook for Reading German Texts*, Langenscheidt, Berlin and Munich 1985

Grammar and Word Formation

The short explanations of points of grammar and word formation in chapters 1 to 3 and 5 include exercises. They are intended to be gone through during the lesson and then discussed. Where the participant is referred to passages in the "Grammar Handbook" these should be looked up and read through in class. If the participants lack experience of using grammars and dictionaries more time should be devoted to this activity.

From chapter 6 onwards, that is to say from about the 12th session, these passages from the textbook and from the "Grammar Handbook" should be read through at home after the text has been gone through. In the next session any questions which have arisen can be dealt with before the next text is tackled.

Revision

In courses which only have a limited number of sessions (2–6) per week it is a good idea to read the text once again at the beginning of the lesson and to repeat one or two of the exercises before moving on to the next text.

What is the aim of the course?

After participating in an introductory course of this sort a reader should be able to independently tackle texts from his particular subject field which are of interest to him. He will, of course, still have to make frequent use of his dictionary and his grammar. Only when he has read a great deal will he be able to dispense with these aids.

Einführung

Wer kann mit diesem Buch arbeiten?

Das Buch gibt eine Einführung für englischsprachige Leser, die Fachzeitschriften und -bücher aus den Bereichen der Geistes- und Sozialwissenschaften in deutscher Sprache lesen wollen. Es setzt Erfahrungen im Lesen englischer Sachprosa voraus. Dagegen sind Kenntnisse in speziellen Fächern und Kenntnis der deutschen Sprache nicht notwendig.

Es ist für den Unterricht in einem Lesekurs gedacht. Der Kurs sollte auf keinen Fall mehr als 20 Teilnehmer haben.

Wieviel Zeit braucht man?

Das Buch ist in 60 Sitzungen zu je 45 Minuten durchzuarbeiten, wenn die Kursteilnehmer bereit sind, den behandelten Stoff zu Hause noch einmal durchzugehen.

Was enthält das Buch?

Das Buch führt in das Lesen von deutschen Sachtexten ein. Die 25 Kapitel enthalten eine Auswahl von Texten aus Buchkatalogen, Verlagsanzeigen, Aufsätzen, Vorträgen und Büchern. Die Texte stammen überwiegend aus den Geistes- und Sozialwissenschaften. Sie sind nach dem Grad der Schwierigkeit für englischsprachige Leser angeordnet.

Den Texten sind kurze Hinweise zu dem Kontext, aus dem sie stammen, und die Quellenangaben vorangestellt, um dem Leser einen Orientierungsrahmen zu geben.

Dann folgen Aufgaben zur schrittweise immer detaillierteren Erschließung der Texte und zuletzt kurze Darstellungen der relevanten Grammatik- und Wortbildungsphänomene anhand von Beispielen aus den vorangegangenen Texten.

Ausführlichere Darstellungen zu Grammatik und Wortbildung sind in dem Band „Grammar Handbook"* zu finden, auf den sich alle Verweise im Buch beziehen.

Das Buch ist kontrastiv angelegt. Es stützt sich auf die lexikalischen und strukturellen Ähnlichkeiten der deutschen und der englischen Sprache sowie auf die inhaltlichen und formalen Gemeinsamkeiten in der Sachprosa.

Im ersten und zweiten Kapitel werden deutsche und englische Wörter germanischen Ursprungs (sog. Cognates) miteinander verglichen, Ähnlichkeiten und Unterschiede aufgezeigt.

Im zweiten Kapitel wird eine weitere Gemeinsamkeit hervorgehoben, nämlich die große Anzahl gemeinsamer Begriffe lateinischen und griechischen Ursprungs (sog. internationale Wörter).

Die Texte der Kapitel 1−4 sind Buchtitel, Überschriften, Inhaltsverzeichnisse, Legenden zu Abbildungen. In diesen Textsorten überwiegen Nominalphrasen. Erfahrungsgemäß ist es nützlich, Nominalphrasen zunächst isoliert, d. h. außerhalb eines Satzrahmens, zu erfassen.

Gleichzeitig erscheinen in diesen ersten Kapiteln zahlreiche Grundwörter und die häufigsten Funktionswörter in typischen Zusammenhängen. Einige der Grundwörter treten auch in exemplarischen Ableitungen und Zusammensetzungen auf.

In den Kapiteln 5−8 kommen die ersten beschreibenden Texte hinzu, zunächst aus ein oder zwei einfachen Sätzen bestehend. Sie zeigen die für die Sachprosa charakteristischen Verbformen der 3. Person im Präsens.

Die Kapitel 9−25 enthalten Ausschnitte aus verschiedenen längeren Texten. Kapitel 16 bringt die Fortsetzung des Textes von

Kapitel 15. Kapitel 17 schließt sich thematisch an. Die drei letzten Kapitel, 23−25, enthalten drei Abschnitte aus einem Text. An diesen kapitelübergreifenden längeren Texten zeigt sich, wenn auch nur ansatzweise, der Effekt des Weiterlesens: Man liest sich zunehmend in ein Thema ein und versteht auf der Grundlage des bekannten den folgenden Textabschnitt wesentlich leichter.

Wie arbeitet man mit dem Buch?

Texte

Die Hinweise zum Text und die Quellenangaben werden gelesen, um sich im voraus über den Text zu orientieren.

Der deutsche Text wird zwei- bis dreimal vom Lehrer ganz vorgelesen, im üblichen Vortragstempo. − Wenn die technischen Möglichkeiten vorhanden sind, sollte der Lehrer jeden Text auch auf Tonband oder Kassette sprechen und die Aufnahmen den Kursteilnehmern für die häusliche Arbeit zur Verfügung stellen. Während des Vorlesens lesen die Kursteilnehmer im Buch still mit. Wenn sie den Text gleichzeitig hören und sehen, erkennen sie an der Intonation und Akzentuierung die inhaltlichen Einheiten und die wesentlichen Informationsträger. Das Schriftbild neuer Wörter und Strukturen prägt sich dem Gedächtnis besser ein, wenn es durch das Lautbild ergänzt wird.

Schriftliche Aufgaben

Jede schriftliche Aufgabe wird zuerst von den Kursteilnehmern selbständig, d. h. allein oder auch in Partner- oder Gruppenarbeit, ausgeführt. Anschließend werden die Lösungen besprochen. Eventuell aufgetretene Schwierigkeiten werden dabei geklärt. Erst danach geht man an die nächste Aufgabe.

Bei Aufgaben, wo aus dem Text zitiert werden soll, ist es nützlich, die gefundenen Lösungen an die Tafel oder am Tageslichtprojektor auf die Folie zu schreiben, um sie gemeinsam zu besprechen. Bei der Besprechung werden die Zitate und die vorgegebenen englischen Entsprechungen kritisch miteinander verglichen, um zu einem genauen Verständnis der betreffenden Textstellen zu gelangen.

Auf deutsch zu schreiben sind entweder Grundformen aus dem Wörterbuch oder einzelne Ausdrücke und kurze Sätze aus dem Text, und zwar nur in den Formen, wie sie im Buch zu finden sind, d. h. sie sind abzuschreiben, als wörtliche Zitate.

Das Abschreiben hilft ebenfalls, den neuen Stoff besser im Gedächtnis zu behalten.

Mündliche Aufgaben

Aufgaben, die mündlich zu lösen sind, werden ebenfalls zuerst von den Kursteilnehmern untereinander besprochen und soweit wie möglich geklärt. Der Lehrer greift ein, falls keine befriedigende Klärung erreicht wird oder auch, falls die Diskussion zu weit vom Thema wegführt.

Es wird nicht gefordert, daß die Kursteilnehmer deutsch sprechen. Sie werden jedoch, anfangs nur gelegentlich, ab Kapitel 7 zunehmend, wörtlich aus dem deutschen Text zu zitieren haben. Die Aussprache sollte verständlich sein, auf Korrektheit kommt es dabei nicht an.

Das Vorlesen einzelner Ausdrücke oder Satzteile, d. h. sie auszusprechen, trägt dazu bei, sie besser im Gedächtnis zu behalten.

Grammatik und Wortbildung

In den Kapiteln 1−3 und 5 enthalten die Darstellungen zu

---

*Hanna Rogalla, Willy Rogalla: *Grammar Handbook for Reading German Texts*, Langenscheidt, Berlin und München 1985.

7

Grammatik und Wortbildung Aufgaben. Sie sind im Unterricht zu lösen und dann zu besprechen. Auch die dazu angegebenen Passagen im „Grammar Handbook" sind im Unterricht nachzuschlagen und zu lesen. Man sollte darauf mehr Zeit verwenden, wenn die Kursteilnehmer im Gebrauch von Grammatik und Wörterbuch noch ungeübt sind.

Ab Kapitel 6, etwa nach der 12. Sitzung, sollten diese Passagen in Textbuch und „Grammar Handbook", jeweils nach Abschluß der Textlektüre, zu Hause durchgelesen werden. In der folgenden Sitzung können dabei aufgetretene Fragen geklärt werden, bevor der nächste Text bearbeitet wird.

Wiederholen

In Kursen mit wenigen Sitzungen (2–6) pro Woche ist es nützlich, am Beginn der Sitzung den letzten Text noch einmal durchzulesen und ein oder zwei von den Aufgaben zu wiederholen, bevor man mit dem neuen Text anfängt.

Was ist das Ziel?

Nach einem solchen einführenden Kurs sollte ein Leser imstande sein, deutsche Texte aus seinem Fachbereich, die ihn interessieren, selbständig durchzulesen. Natürlich wird er noch häufig Wörterbuch und Grammatik benutzen müssen. Erst wenn er viel gelesen hat, wird er auf diese Hilfsmittel verzichten können.

Contents

* Titel nicht original

Text

Shakespeare

1 Antonius und Cleopatra
2 Ende gut, alles gut
3 Julius Cäsar
4 Der Kaufmann von Venedig
5 Die Komödie der Irrungen
6 König Lear
7 König Richard III.
8 Die lustigen Weiber von Windsor
9 Maß für Maß
10 Romeo und Julia
11 Ein Sommernachtstraum
12 Der Sturm
13 Timon von Athen
14 Viel Lärm um nichts
15 Das Wintermärchen

Text: Titles of plays by Shakespeare, and a quotation from Hamlet.

Source: Book catalogues.

Task 1:
Listen and follow the text; read the text through again and enter the corresponding German titles in the gaps next to the English ones.

Shakespeare

a *All's Well That Ends Well*

b *Antony and Cleopatra*

c *The Comedy of Errors*

d *Julius Caesar*

e *King Lear*

f *Measure for Measure*

g *The Merchant of Venice*

h *The Merry Wives of Windsor*

i *A Midsummer Night's Dream*

k *Much Ado About Nothing*

l *Richard III*

m *Romeo and Juliet*

n *The Tempest*

o *Timon of Athens*

p *The Winter's Tale*

Hamlet: To be, or not to be, that is the question: –
From: Hamlet, Prince of Denmark

Hamlet: Sein oder Nicht sein, das ist die Frage: –

Aus: Hamlet

1

Task 2:
Complete the German versions of the titles, then enter the words which you have filled in in the vocabulary column.

_____ Komödie der Irrungen   *(the = _____)*

_____ lustigen Weiber von Windsor   *(the = _____)*

_____ Kaufmann von Venedig   *(the = _____)*

_____ Wintermärchen   *(the = _____)*

..., _____ ist die Frage.   *(that = _____)*

Timon _____ Athens   *(of = _____)*

Die lustigen Weiber _____ Windsor   *(of = _____)*

Die Komödie _____ Irrungen   *(of = _____)*

_____ Sommernachtstraum   *(a = _____)*

Ende_____, alles _____   *(well = _____)*

_____ Lärm um _____   *(much = _____;*

    nothing = _____)

_____ für _____   *(measure = _____)*

Sein _____ _____ sein –   *(or = _____;*

    not = _____)

das ist die _____.   *(question = _____)*

Note*:
In the German version there are four letters which do not exist in English: $ä$, $ö$, $ü$, $ß$. In which words? How are these letters pronounced? (See *Alphabet*, p. 8, and *Pronunciation*, p. 8.) – Which words are capitalized in German? (See *Spelling*, p. 15.)

Cognates

Task 3:
Read through *Cognates*, pp. 114–115, then write the corresponding German words (in parentheses) in front of the English words.

a _____ *black;* _____ *blue;* _____ *brown;* _____ *green;* _____ *grey;* _____ *red;* _____ *white;*

_____ *yellow* (blau – braun – gelb – grau – grün – rot – schwarz – weiß)

b _____ *broad;* _____ *thick;* _____ *thin;* _____ *round;* _____ *false;* _____ *right;* _____ *fresh;*

_____ *new* (breit – dick – dünn – falsch – frisch – neu – richtig – rund)

c _____ *free;* _____ *rich;* _____ *hot;* _____ *cool;* _____ *earnest;* _____ *fine;* _____ *double;*

_____ *near* (doppelt – ernst – fein – frei – heiß – kühl – nahe – reich)

d _____ *one;* _____ *two;* _____ *three;* _____ *four;* _____ *five;* _____ *six;* _____ *seven;*

_____ *eight;* _____ *nine* (acht – drei – eins – fünf – neun – sechs – sieben – vier – zwei)

e _____ *ten;* _____ *eleven;* _____ *twelve;* _____ *thirteen;* _____ *fifteen;*

_____ *twenty;* _____ *fifty;* _____ *hundred;* _____ *thousand*
(dreizehn – elf – fünfzehn – fünfzig – hundert – tausend – zehn – zwanzig – zwölf)

f _____ *day;* _____ *week;* _____ *month;* _____ *year;* _____ *century* (Jahr – Jahrhundert – Monat – Tag – Woche)

g _____ *east and west;* _____ *north or south* (Norden – oder – Osten – Süden – und – Westen)

---

* All references to: *Grammar Handbook for Reading German Texts* by Hanna Rogalla and Willy Rogalla, Langenscheidt, Berlin, München 1985.

16

Grammar

Basic forms

Task 4:
Look at *Umlaute*, p. 13. Then reduce the nouns (a), adjectives (b) and verbs (c) to their basic forms. Look up these basic forms in the *Basic Word List*. Write them and their English equivalents following the examples given in the space provided.

a **Nouns**

(Plural)   (Singular)

Hände   *hands*   Hand   *hand*

Plätze _____ _____ _____

Bände _____ _____ _____

Schlüsse _____ _____ _____

Töne _____ _____ _____

Gründe _____ _____ _____

b **Adjectives**

(Comparative)   (Positive)

jünger   *younger*   jung   *young*

näher _____ _____ _____

öfter _____ _____ _____

älter _____ _____ _____

c **Verbs**

(Present tense, singular)   (Infinitive)

er läuft   *he runs*   laufen   *to run*

er empfängt   *he* _____ _____ *to* _____

er behält   *he* _____ _____ *to* _____

er läßt   *he* _____ _____ *to* _____

er wächst   *he* _____ _____ *to* _____

1

Word formation

Basic words

Task 5:
Look at *Umlaute*, p. 13. Then reduce the following derivatives to their basic words. Look up these basic words in the *Basic Word List*. Write them and their English equivalents following the examples given in the space provided.

a   (Derivative adjectives)   (Basic nouns)

   stündlich   *hourly*   Stunde   *hour*

   wörtlich   *literal(ly)*   _____   _____

   abendländisch *occidental*   _____   _____

   anfänglich   *initial(ly)*   _____   _____

   zukünftig   *future*   _____   _____

b   (Derivative verbs)   (Basic nouns)

   wählen   *to choose/elect* Wahl   *choice/election*

   strömen   *to stream*   _____   _____

   drücken   *to press*   _____   _____

   färben   *to colour*   _____   _____

   gefährden   *to endanger*   _____   _____

Task 6:
Find the English equivalents of the following German words and write them in the space provided.

	(Adjective)	(Comparative)	(Verb)	(Noun)
a	hoch	höher	erhöhen	Höhe
	high	_____	*to heighten*	*height*
b	lang	länger	verlängern	Länge
	_____	_____	_____	*length*
c	stark	stärker	stärken	Stärke
	_____	*stronger*	_____	_____
d	schwach	schwächer	schwächen	Schwäche
	_____	_____	*to weaken*	_____

Text

Text: Titles of plays by contemporary American playwrights.

Source: Reference books.

> 1 Alle Kinder Gottes haben Flügel
> 2 Alle meine Söhne
> 3 Alles im Garten
> 4 Der amerikanische Traum
> 5 Der haarige Affe
> 6 Die Katze auf dem heißen Blechdach
> 7 Die tätowierte Rose
> 8 Die Zoogeschichte
> 9 Eines langen Tages Reise in die Nacht
> 10 Nach dem Sündenfall
> 11 Requiem für eine Nonne
> 12 Schau heimwärts, Engel!
> 13 Und plötzlich im letzten Sommer

Task:

Read through the German titles and guess at their meaning; then compare and match the German with the English titles; write down the German under the English ones.

a *The Hairy Ape (Eugene O'Neill)*

b *All God's Chillun Got Wings (E. O'Neill)*

c *Long Day's Journey into Night (E. O'Neill)*

d *The Rose Tattoo (Tennessee Williams)*

e *Cat on a Hot Tin Roof (T. Williams)*

f *Suddenly Last Summer (T. Williams)*

g *Look Homeward, Angel! (Thomas Wolfe)*

h *All My Sons (Arthur Miller)*

i *After the Fall (A. Miller)*

j *Requiem for a Nun (William Faulkner)*

k *The Zoo-Story (Edward Albee)*

l *The American Dream (E. Albee)*

m *Everything in the Garden (E. Albee)*

Text: Publisher's notice for a paperback encyclopedia.

Source: Fischer Taschenbuch 851, Fischer Taschenbuch Verlag, Frankfurt/M.

Das Fischer Lexikon
ENZYKLOPÄDIE DES WISSENS

1 Die nichtchristlichen Religionen	24 Geschichte
2 Staat und Politik	25 Sprachen
3 Christliche Religion	26 Chemie
4 Astronomie	27 Biologie I Botanik
5 Musik	28 Biologie II Zoologie
6 Psychologie	29/1 Mathematik I
7 Internationale Beziehungen	29/2 Mathematik II
8 Wirtschaft	30 Technik I Bautechnik
9 Publizistik (in Vorbereitung)	31 Technik II Maschinenbau
10 Soziologie	32 Technik III Elektrische Energietechnik
11 Philosophie	33 Technik IV Elektrische Nachrichtentechnik
12 Recht	34 Literatur I
13 Völkerkunde	35/1,2 Literatur II/III
14 Geographie	36 Pädagogik
15 Anthropologie	37 Geschichte in Gestalten I
16 Medizin I	38 Geschichte in Gestalten II
17 Medizin II	39 Geschichte in Gestalten III
18 Medizin III	40 Geschichte in Gestalten IV
19 Physik	
20 Geophysik	
21 Bildende Kunst I	
22 Bildende Kunst II	
23 Bildende Kunst III	

Fischer Bücherei

Task:

Underline the words which are close to English. – What spelling rule can be established for the words next to the numbers 4, 6, 10, 11, 14, 15, and for those next to the numbers 2, 5, 19, 20, 29 when compared to English spelling?

Note:

The differences are greater in pronunciation and stress.

2

Text: Titles of books from different disciplines.

Source: Book catalogues.

Task 1:
Listen and follow the text; read the text through again and underline all those words whose meaning is apparent.

1	**Medizin**	Zollinger, H. U.: Pathologische Anatomie 1 Allgemeine Pathologie 2 Spezielle Pathologie
5	**Chemie**	Fluck, Ekkehard/Brastet, R. C.: Allgemeine und anorganische Chemie Kaufmann, Heinz: Grundlagen der organischen Chemie
10	**Geographie**	Fochler-Hauke, Gustav (Hrsg.): Allgemeine Geographie
	Sprachwissenschaft	Wunderlich, Dieter: Grundlagen der Linguistik
	Musik	Renner, Hans: Grundlagen der Musik
15	**Physik**	Einstein, Albert: Über die spezielle und allgemeine Relativitätstheorie
20		Falk, G.: Theoretische Physik auf der Grundlage einer allgemeinen Dynamik
		Groot, S. R. de: Thermodynamik irreversibler Prozesse
25		– u. Peter Mazur: Methoden der Thermodynamik irreversibler Prozesse
		Traupel, Walter: Die Grundlagen der Thermodynamik
30	**Philosophie**	Körner, Stephan: Grundfragen der Philosophie
		Ortega y Gasset, José: Was ist Philosophie?
		Russell, Bertrand: Probleme der Philosophie

Task 2:
There are two pairs of antonyms in the text. Find and underline them.

Task 3:
Compare the English words with the German ones; write the English equivalents in the space provided; find and compare the appropriate titles in the text.

Anatomie	*anatomy*
speziell	*special (– and the antonym:)*
allgemein	_____
Chemie	_____
anorganisch	_____
Grundlagen	*fundamental principles*
Sprachwissenschaft	_____
Musik	_____
Physik	_____
über	*on, concerning*
Theorie	_____
theoretisch	_____
auf der Grundlage	*on the basis*
Methode	*method*
Methoden	_____
Prozeß	*process*
Prozesse	_____
Frage	_____
Fragen	*questions, problems*
Grundfragen (cf. Grundlagen)	_____
Problem	_____
Probleme	_____
Was ist …?	_____

20

Task 4:
Which of the books from the list deal with subjects similar to those of the following English books? – Suggestion: Copy the answers from the text before discussing them in class.

a *The Problems of Philosophy*

b *Classical Thermodynamics*

c *Fundamental Questions in Philosophy*

d *Textbook of Human Anatomy*

e *The Face of the Earth*

Word formation

"International" words

> Medizin: Pathologische Anatomie, (1) Allgemeine Pathologie
> Allgemeine und anorganische Chemie
> Über die spezielle und allgemeine Relativitätstheorie
> Grundlagen der Linguistik
> Grundlagen der Musik
> Grundlagen der organischen Chemie
> Physik: Thermodynamik irreversibler Prozesse
> Theoretische Physik auf der Grundlage einer allgemeinen Dynamik
> Grundfragen der Philosophie

Words of Latin or Greek origin are often written (and spoken) only slightly differently in German and English (cf. *Foreign Words*, p. 116).

Task 5:
Look for such words in the extract from the text given and write the German equivalents in the space provided. – Suggestion: Practise saying these words in German (with the instructor) with particular attention to stress and pronunciation.

a English *-c-:* *special, medicine, processes* (compare: *place*/Platz)

   German *-z-:*

b English *-c-:* *physics, linguistics, music, dynamics* (compare: *cold*/kalt)

   German *-k-:*

c English *-ic(al):* *pathological, organic, inorganic, theoretical*

   German *-isch:*

d Englisch *-y:* *anatomy, pathology, theory, philosophy*

   German *-ie:*

21

3

Text

Text: Table of Contents from a book summarizing the findings of research into fear.

Source: Walter von Baeyer/Wanda von Baeyer-Katte, Angst, © Suhrkamp Verlag, Frankfurt am Main 1973, S. 5.

Angst

Inhalt

Vorwort 7
Einleitung 9
1 Was ist Angst? 21
2 Zur Biologie und Physiologie der Angst 45
3 Experimentelle Psychologie der Angst 59
4 Soziale Angst 87
5 Terror 120
6 Psychopathologie der Angst 146

Task 1:
Listen and follow the text; underline all those words whose meaning is apparent; try to guess the meaning of the remaining words and/or read them through to yourself again.

Note:
The German expression *Vorwort* does not provide us with any information as to whether it was written by the author of the book or another person. It therefore means *foreword* or *preface*.

Vocabulary:
Since it is stated above that this text is a table of contents *Inhalt*

probably means: _____.

Since the word *Einleitung* comes between *Vorwort* and the title of chapter 1 *Was ist Angst?* it could mean:

_____.

The preposition *zur (zu + der)* means *on (the)*, *concerning (the)*.

Task 2:
Listen and read once again; provide written answers to the questions on the text.

In which part of the book would you expect to find information

a   about tests for measuring fear?

_____

b   about fear of enclosed spaces (claustrophobia)?

_____

c   about fear as a means of intimidation and oppression?

_____

d   about going pale and sweating with fear?

_____

e   about the fear of behaving differently from neighbours or colleagues?

_____

f   In which chapter would you expect to find a definition of fear?

_____

Text: Illustration and caption from a book on the writing, signs and symbols of different peoples.

Quelle: Franz H. Wills, Schrift und Zeichen der Völker, Econ Verlag, Düsseldorf/Wien 1977, S. 148.

Abb. 1 Fabeltier (sibirischer Tiger?) auf der Rückseite eines chinesischen Bronzespiegels (Han-Dynastie, 2. Jahrh. v. d. Ztw.)

Task 1:
Listen and follow the text; read the text through again, then write the answers to questions a and b; discuss the various solutions.

a   Which words in the caption might be composed of two words?

_____

22

b What are the probable English equivalents of the following words and parts of words?

Fabel- _____

sibirischer Tiger _____

auf der -seite _____

eines chinesischen Bronze- _____

Task 2:
Discuss and answer the questions.
a *Tier*: What might this word mean when taken in conjunction with *sibirischer Tiger* and the illustration? (Clue: The cognate word in modern English has a much more limited meaning than the German word.)
b *Spiegel*: What kind of object might be this shape? (Clue: The most influential West-German political magazine is called *Der Spiegel*.)
c *Rück-*: On which side of the Bronze object might we expect to find the *Fabeltier*?
d *2. Jahrh. v. d. Ztw.*: Could this expression refer to a place where, for example, the object was found or is kept? What speaks for this idea? What speaks against it?
e The abbreviation is, written out in full, *zweites Jahrhundert vor der Zeitwende*. What might this possibly mean?
f What is the meaning of the expression *Han-Dynastie*?

Task 3:
Take another look at the illustration and make a list of all the information you now possess about it.

Text: Titles of books from different disciplines.

Source: Book catalogues.

1	**Botanik**	Zimmermann, Walter: Geschichte der Pflanzen
	Musik	Abendroth, Walter: Kurze Geschichte der Musik
5	**Psychologie**	Wertheimer, Michael: Kurze Geschichte der Psychologie
	Technik	Timm, Albrecht: Kleine Geschichte der Technologie
10	**Literaturwissenschaft**	Martini, Fritz: Deutsche Literaturgeschichte
		Laaths, Erwin: Geschichte der Weltliteratur
	Anthropologie	Koenigswald, Gustav H. R. v.: Die Geschichte des Menschen
15	**Biologie**	Hölder, Helmut: Naturgeschichte des Lebens von seinen Anfängen bis zum Menschen
	Philosophie	Châtelet, François (Hrsg.): Geschichte der Philosophie II
20		Die Philosophie des Mittelalters (1.—15. Jahrhundert)

Geschichte	Abendroth, Wolfgang: Sozialgeschichte der europäischen Arbeiterbewegung	
	Binder, Gerhart: Deutsche Geschichte des 20. Jahrhunderts	25
	Elton, G. R.: Europa im Zeitalter der Reformation 1517—1559	
	Grebing, Helga: Geschichte der deutschen Arbeiterbewegung	30
	Pirenne, Henri: Sozial- und Wirtschaftsgeschichte Europas im Mittelalter	
	Ranke, Leopold von: Deutsche Geschichte im Zeitalter der Reformation	35
	Schnabel, Franz: Deutsche Geschichte im 19. Jahrhundert	
	Schulz, Gerhard: Deutschland seit dem Ersten Weltkrieg 1918—1945	40

Task 1:
Listen and follow the text; underline all those words whose meaning is apparent; try to guess the meaning of the remaining words and/or read them through to yourself again.

Task 2:
Compare the English words with the German ones; write the English equivalents in the space provided; find and compare the appropriate titles in the text.

die Geschichte	*history*
die Pflanze (pl.: Pflanzen)	_____ (Botanik!)
kurz	*short, brief*
klein	*small, little*
die Technik	_____ (Technologie!)
die Welt	*world*
der Mensch	_____ (Anthropologie!)
Die Geschichte des Menschen	*History of* _____
das Leben	*life*
der Anfang	*beginning*
von seinen Anfängen	_____ *its origins*
bis zu (zum = zu + article dem)	*up to/down to (the)*
das Alter	*age*
das Mittelalter	_____
das Jahrhundert	_____ *(100 years)*

die Arbeit	*work, labour*	im Zeitalter der Reformation	_____ *of the Reformation*
der Arbeiter	_____	die Wirtschaft	*economy; industry and commerce*
die Bewegung	*movement*	die Geschichte Europas	_____ *Europe*
sozial	_____	im 19. Jahrhundert	_____
des 20. Jahrhunderts	*of the* _____	der Krieg	_____
die Zeit	*time*	seit dem Ersten Weltkrieg	*since the First* _____
in (im = in + article dem)	*in*		

Task 3:
What book or books in the list would you consult

a   if you wanted to find out about German contemporary history?

   _____

b   if you were interested in the German poet J. W. Goethe?

   _____

c   if you were looking for information about the German workers' movement?

   _____

d   if you wanted to get a general view of the development of plants?

   _____

Suggestion: Copy the answers from the text before discussing them in class.

Task 4:
In which of the German books in the list would you find topics similar to those in the following English titles?

a   *Technology in the Ancient World*

   _____

b   *Germany in Our Time*

   _____

c   *Short History of Western Music*

   _____

d   *Short History of the British Working-Class Movement*

   _____

e   *The Medieval Economy and Society*

   _____

Suggestion: Copy the answers from the text before discussing them in class.

Word formation
Compound words (nouns)

Task 5:
Look for compound words in the list (p. 23) and write them in the
space provided (cf. *Compound Words*, pp. 120–123).

a   Wissenschaft:

b   Literatur:

c   Bewegung:

d   Alter:

e   Geschichte:

Text

Text: Illustration with caption from a book on psychology taken from the section dealing with theories of learning.

Quelle: Charlotte Bühler, Psychologie im Leben unserer Zeit, Droemer Knaur Verlag, München/Zürich 1962, zit. nach Knaur Taschenbuch, Band 269, München/Zürich 1972, S. 47.

Abb. 2   Das Labyrinth von Small, 1901

Abb. 3   Eine Ratte beim Lernversuch im Labyrinth

Text: Illustration with caption from a book on psychology taken from the section dealing with ageing.

Quelle: Charlotte Bühler, a. a. O., S. 18.

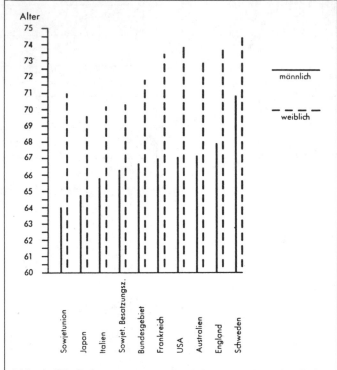

Abb. 4   Die Lebenserwartung in einigen Ländern der Erde. (Vereinfacht nach „Wirtschaft und Statistik", 1961)

Vocabulary:
beim (contraction of *bei dem*) – *at the, in the course of the*
im (contraction of *in dem*) – *in the*

Task 1:
Look at the illustration; listen and read to yourself; reproduce the information contained in the text.

Task 2:
Discuss the possible meanings of *Versuch*.

Task 1:
Look at the table; listen and follow the text; discuss the questions.
a   What do the numbers 60–75 refer to in the table?
b   What do the continuous vertical lines signify?
c   Which two names of countries are hard to understand? Which countries might they refer to, bearing in mind that this is an extract form a West German book published in 1961? (*Sowjet. Besatzungsz.* is, written in full, *Sowjetische Besatzungszone.*)

Task 2:
Write the English equivalents under the German words.

Die Lebens-   in   einigen Ländern   der Erde

_____ —— *some* _____ _____

Vereinfacht nach „Wirtschaft und Statistik", 1961

Simplified from _____ _____ _____ *1961*

Task 3:
What does *Erwartung* probably mean?

Note:
Until about 1970 the *Deutsche Demokratische Republik (German Democratic Republic)* was referred to as the *Sowjetzone, Sowjetische Besatzungszone, Ostzone* or *Mitteldeutschland.*

Text: In the summer of 1946 the physicist and philosopher *von Weizsäcker* held twelve lectures on *The History of Nature.* Two years later these lectures were published in book-form. The text which follows is the list of contents from this book.

Quelle: Carl Friedrich von Weizsäcker, Die Geschichte der Natur, Vandenhoeck & Ruprecht, Göttingen 1964, S. 4.

INHALT

I. Einleitung 5
II. Rückgang in die Geschichte der Erde 14
III. Die räumliche Struktur des Kosmos 24
IV. Die zeitliche Struktur des Kosmos 31
V. Unendlichkeit 43
VI. Sternsysteme 53
VII. Sterne 66
VIII. Die Erde 75
IX. Das Leben 83
X. Die Seele 95
XI. Der Mensch. Äußere Geschichte 104
XII. Der Mensch. Innere Geschichte. 114
Anmerkungen 127
Zeittafeln 129
Tafel zur räumlichen Struktur des Kosmos 132
Geologisch-Paläontologische Zeittafel 133

Task 1:
Listen and follow the text; underline all those words whose meaning is apparent; try to guess the meaning of the remaining words and/or read them through to yourself again.

Task 2:
Enter the corresponding English expressions in the gaps provided; find the relevant parts of the text and compare them with your answers; discuss the solutions.

die Geschichte der Natur	______
der Inhalt	______
die Einleitung	______
die Erde	______
die Geschichte der Erde	______
der Rückgang (look up Gang in the *Basic Word List;* Rück- as in Rückseite eines Bronzespiegels)	______
Rückgang in die Geschichte	______
die Struktur des Kosmos	______
die Zeit	______
die zeitliche Struktur	______
die räumliche Struktur (Zeit und Raum are the two categories which go together)	______
die Unendlichkeit (das Ende – endlich – unendlich – Unendlichkeit like *end – finite* – . . .)	______
der Stern (comes between Kosmos/Unendlichkeit and Erde/Mensch; cognate)	______
das Sternsystem	______
das Leben	______
die Seele (comes between Erde/Leben and Mensch; cognate)	______
innere Geschichte	______
äußere Geschichte (antonyms: innere – äußere)	______
die Anmerkung	*note, comment*
die Tafel	______
die Zeittafel	______
Tafel zur Struktur des Kosmos	______

Task 3:
Answer the questions.

a How is the series of lectures arranged? What progression does the author have in mind?

b Which lecture (or lectures) does/do not seem to you to fall strictly within the framework of the natural sciences?

Suggestion: Practise saying these words and phrases in German (with the instructor) with particular attention to stress and pronunciation.

5

Text

Text: Two quotations from Greek philosophers.

Quelle: Georg Büchmann, Geflügelte Worte, Haude & Spener, Berlin 1972.

> Der Mensch ist das Maß aller Dinge.
> Protagoras
> Nach Heraklit ist der Krieg der Vater aller Dinge.

_____ *measure*

_____ *things*

Task 1:
Listen and follow the text; enter the German expressions in the gaps next to the English ones.

Task 2:
Answer the questions.
a   Who are the authors of the quotations?
b   How does German indicate that someone is being quoted? Which expressions might be used in English to indicate the same?

Text: Titles of books and short summaries of their contents.

Quelle: Publishers' catalogues.

> Klaus von Beyme
> **Die politischen Theorien der Gegenwart**
> Dieses Buch gibt vom Standpunkt des Methodenpluralismus einen systematischen Überblick über die politischen Theorien des 20. Jahrhunderts.

_____ *gives*

_____ *present (i. e. 20. Jahrhundert)*

_____ *survey*

_____ *this*

> Jakob Grimm
> **Deutsche Mythologie**
> In diesem Werk behandelt Grimm das religiöse Leben der germanischen Völker.

_____ *peoples*

_____ *treats, deals with*

> **Psychologisches Wörterbuch**
> Herausgegeben von Friedrich Dorsch
> Dieses Wörterbuch informiert und orientiert über das Gesamtgebiet der Psychologie, insbesondere über Denken, Lernen, Motivation, Psycholinguistik und Pädagogische Psychologie.

_____ *dictionary*

_____ *edited by*

_____ *in particular, especially*

_____ *the whole (entire) field*

_____ *thinking*

Task 3:
Listen and follow the text; enter the German expressions in the gaps next to the English ones.

Task 4:
Answer the questions

on the book by *Klaus von Beyme*:

a   What is the main topic of *Beyme*'s book?
b   In what form does he present the political theories?
c   From which particular standpoint does he deal with the topic?

on the book by *Jakob Grimm*:

d   What is *Grimm*'s *German Mythology* about?
e   The book appeared in 1835. Do you think that the title and the publisher's notice are in agreement with one another? Which title might a contemporary scientist have preferred?

on the psychological dictionary:

f   Who might be interested in this dictionary apart from psychologists and why?

Task 5:
Underline the verbs in the five sentences. In which sentences is the verb in a different position to what it would be in English?

a   Der Mensch ist das Maß aller Dinge.
b   Nach Heraklit ist der Krieg der Vater aller Dinge.
c   Dieses Buch gibt vom Standpunkt des Methodenpluralismus einen systematischen Überblick über die politischen Theorien des 20. Jahrhunderts.
d   In diesem Werk behandelt Grimm das religiöse Leben der germanischen Völker.
e   Dieses Wörterbuch informiert und orientiert über das Gesamtgebiet der Psychologie, insbesondere über Denken, Lernen, Motivation, Psycholinguistik und Pädagogische Psychologie.

Text: Titles of works by Einstein, titles of works about Einstein, biographical data.

Quelle: Book catalogues, reference books.

Task 1:
Listen and follow the text; read the text through again and underline all those words whose meaning is apparent; try to guess the meaning of the remaining words and/or read them through to yourself again.

1	Autor: *Albert Einstein* (1879–1955), deutsch-amerikanischer Physiker
	Aufsätze:
5	– Zur allgemeinen Relativitätstheorie (1915) – Die Grundlage der allgemeinen Relativitätstheorie (1916) – Über die spezielle und allgemeine Relativitätstheorie (1916)
10	Sekundärliteratur: *Max Born*: Die Relativitätstheorie Einsteins und ihre physikalischen Grundlagen (^{3}1922) *Ph. Frank*: Einstein, sein Leben und seine Zeit (1949) *L. Infeld*: Albert Einstein, sein Werk und sein Einfluß auf
15	unsere Welt (deutsch 1957) *Bertrand Russell*: Das ABC der Relativitätstheorie (deutsch 1970)
	Anmerkungen: *Max Born* (1882–1970), deutscher Kernphysiker
20	*Leopold Infeld* (1898–1968), polnischer Physiker *Bertrand Russell* (1872–1970), englischer Philosoph, Mathematiker und Schriftsteller

Task 2:
Enter the corresponding English expressions in the gaps provided; find the relevant parts of the text and compare them with your answers; discuss the solutions.

der Autor	_____
der Physiker	_____
die Physik	_____
Aufsätze	*essays*
zur (contraction of zu der)	*on (the), concerning (the)*
über die	*on (the), concerning (the)*
speziell	_____
allgemein	_____
die Grundlage	_____
sekundär	_____

das Leben	*life*
die Zeit	*time*
sein Werk	_____ *work*
Einfluß auf	*influence* _____
unsere Welt	*our* _____
der Kern	*nucleus* (also *core; kernel*)
der Kernphysiker	*nuclear* _____
der Mathematiker	_____
der Schriftsteller	*writer, author*
der Philosoph	_____
die Philosophie	_____

Text: Titles of works by Goethe and about him.

Quelle: Book catalogues, reference books.

Task 1:
Listen and follow the text; read the text through again and underline all those words whose meaning is apparent; try to guess the meaning of the remaining words and/or read them through to yourself again.

Autor: *Johann Wolfgang von Goethe* (1749–1832), deutscher Lyriker, Dramatiker, Romanschriftsteller, Philosoph, Politiker und Wissenschaftler	1
aus seinen Werken: – Schriften zur Geologie, Mineralogie – Schriften zur Botanik und Wissenschaftslehre – Schriften zur vergleichenden Anatomie, zur Zoologie und zur Physiognomik – Zur Farbenlehre. Didaktischer Teil – Materialien zur Geschichte der Farbenlehre	5 10
aus der Sekundärliteratur: *Karl Goedeke*: Goethes Leben und Schriften (1874) *Alexander Baumgartner*: Goethe. Sein Leben und seine Werke (^{2}1885–1886) *Hermann Siebeck*: Goethe als Denker (1902) *Hermann Glockner*: Das philosophische Problem in Goethes Farbenlehre (1924) *Werner Heisenberg*: Die Goethesche und die Newtonsche Farbenlehre im Lichte der modernen Physik (1941) *Martin Gebhardt*: Goethe als Physiker (1932) *Hermann v. Helmholtz*: Goethes naturwissenschaftliche Arbeiten (1853) *Hans Fischer*: Goethes Naturwissenschaft (1950) *Berthold Litzmann*: Goethes Lyrik (1903) *Victor Hehn*: Gedanken über Goethe (1886)	15 20 25

```
1   Autor:
    Johann Wolfgang von Goethe (1749–1832), deutscher Lyri-
        ker, Dramatiker, Romanschriftsteller, Philosoph, Politiker
        und Wissenschaftler

5   aus seinen Werken:
        – Schriften zur Geologie, Mineralogie
        – Schriften zur Botanik und Wissenschaftslehre
        – Schriften zur vergleichenden Anatomie, zur Zoologie
          und zur Physiognomik
10      – Zur Farbenlehre. Didaktischer Teil
        – Materialien zur Geschichte der Farbenlehre

    aus der Sekundärliteratur:
        Karl Goedeke: Goethes Leben und Schriften (1874)
15      Alexander Baumgartner: Goethe. Sein Leben und seine
            Werke (²1885–1886)
        Hermann Siebeck: Goethe als Denker (1902)
        Hermann Glockner: Das philosophische Problem in Goe-
            thes Farbenlehre (1924)
20      Werner Heisenberg: Die Goethesche und die Newtonsche
            Farbenlehre im Lichte der modernen Physik (1941)
        Martin Gebhardt: Goethe als Physiker (1932)
        Hermann v. Helmholtz: Goethes naturwissenschaftliche
            Arbeiten (1853)
25      Hans Fischer: Goethes Naturwissenschaft (1950)
        Berthold Litzmann: Goethes Lyrik (1903)
        Victor Hehn: Gedanken über Goethe (1886)
```

die Farbe	*colour*
_____	*theory of colours*
der Teil	*part*
_____	*materials*
_____	*history*
_____	*his life and his works*
_____	*thinker*
denken	*to think*
_____	*in the light of modern physics*
_____	*physicist*
die Arbeit	*work*
_____	*Goethe's scientific works*
_____	*natural science*
_____	*thoughts* (see above: *to think*)

Task 2:
Find the relevant parts of the text and enter the corresponding German expressions in the gaps provided.

_____	*author*
_____	*poet*
der Roman	*novel*
_____	*novelist*
_____	*philosopher*
_____	*scientist*
_____	*writings*
die Lehre	*theory*
_____	*science theory*
_____	*on comparative anatomy*
vergleichen	*to compare*

Task 3:
Find the answers in the text and enter them in the gaps provided.

a Which of the listed works by *Goethe* deal with an area or subject similar to that of the following?

Isaac Newton: Opticks or a Treatise of the Reflections, Refractions, Inflections and Colours of Light (1704)

Arthur Schopenhauer: Über das Sehn und die Farben (1816)

J. W. v. Goethe: _____

Charles Darwin: On the Origin of Species (1859)

J. W. v. Goethe: _____

b In which work among the listed secondary literature would you *not* look for references to *Goethe*'s scientific work?

_____

Grammar

1 Verb forms

Present, 3rd person singular		Infinitive of the verb	
ist	*is*	sein	*to be*
gibt	*gives*	geben	*to give*
behandelt	*deals with*	behandeln	*to deal with*
informiert	*informs*	informieren	*to inform*
orientiert	*orientates*	orientieren	*to orientate*

In the 3rd person singular of the present tense verbs have the ending *-t* (comparable to the ending *-s* in English).

The infinitive is the basic form of the verb. This is the form in which verbs appear in dictionaries. It ends in *-en* or *-n*.

2 Singular and plural forms of nouns

In English, plural nouns are nearly always characterized by the ending *-s* or *-es*. In German, there are several plural indicators, e. g. *-en, -n, -e, -er*, or *Umlaut*, a modified vowel, but hardly ever *-s*. (See *Nouns: Plural*, p. 22ff.)

Task 4:
Read through the extracts from the texts given below and underline the plural nouns. Identify the plural indicators and write them in the gaps provided.

singular

a Schriften zur Botanik und Wissenschaftslehre — die Schrift
Goethes naturwissenschaftliche Arbeiten — die Arbeit
Internationale Beziehungen — die Beziehung

The plural ends in _____.

b Geschichte der Pflanzen — die Pflanze
Grundfragen der Philosophie — die Frage
Gedanken über Goethe — der Gedanke
Die politischen Theorien der Gegenwart — die Theorie

The plural ends in _____.

c Probleme der Philosophie — das Problem
Goethe. Sein Leben und seine Werke — das Werk
Alle meine Söhne — der Sohn
Aufsätze von Albert Einstein — der Aufsatz

The plural (frequently with an *Umlaut*) ends in _____.

d Alle Kinder Gottes haben Flügel — das Kind
Psychologisches Wörterbuch — das Wort
Das religiöse Leben der germanischen Völker — das Volk

The plural (frequently with an *Umlaut*) ends in _____.

Masculine and neuter nouns ending in *-er, -el, -en* in the singular have the same ending in the plural:

Geschichte der deutschen Arbeiterbewegung — der Arbeiter
Alle Kinder Gottes haben Flügel — der Flügel

Which plural forms would you expect for the nouns der Physiker, der Mathematiker, der Wissenschaftler?

3 Genitive case

In German the noun ending *-s* (or *-es*) indicates the genitive case of masculine and neuter nouns. The definite article in this case is *des*.

Task 5:
Read through the extracts from the texts given below and underline the masculine and neuter nouns in the genitive case.

Deutsche Geschichte des 20. Jahrhunderts
Naturgeschichte des Lebens
Die Philosophie des Mittelalters
Sozial- und Wirtschaftsgeschichte Europas im Mittelalter
Die Relativitätstheorie Einsteins und ihre physikalischen Grundlagen
Goethes Leben und Schriften
Die Geschichte des Menschen*

(See *Nouns: Case, Genitive*, p. 21, and *Nouns: Declension*, p. 26.)

Feminine and plural nouns take no ending in the genitive case. The definite article in this case is *der*.

Task 6:
Read through the extracts from the texts given below and underline the feminine and plural nouns in the genitive case.

Grundlagen der organischen Chemie
Probleme der Philosophie
Geschichte der Pflanzen
Geschichte der deutschen Arbeiterbewegung
Europa im Zeitalter der Reformation 1517−1559
Die Grundlage der allgemeinen Relativitätstheorie
Materialien zur Geschichte der Farbenlehre

*Nouns like *der Mensch* take *-en* instead of *-es* in the genitive case.

6

Text

Text: Illustrations with captions.

Quelle: Franz H. Wills, Schrift und Zeichen der Völker, Econ Verlag, Düsseldorf/Wien 1977, S. 114, 131 (Abb. 5 und 6). Erwin Laaths, Geschichte der Weltliteratur, Droemersche Verlagsanstalt, München 1953, S. 461 (Abb.7).

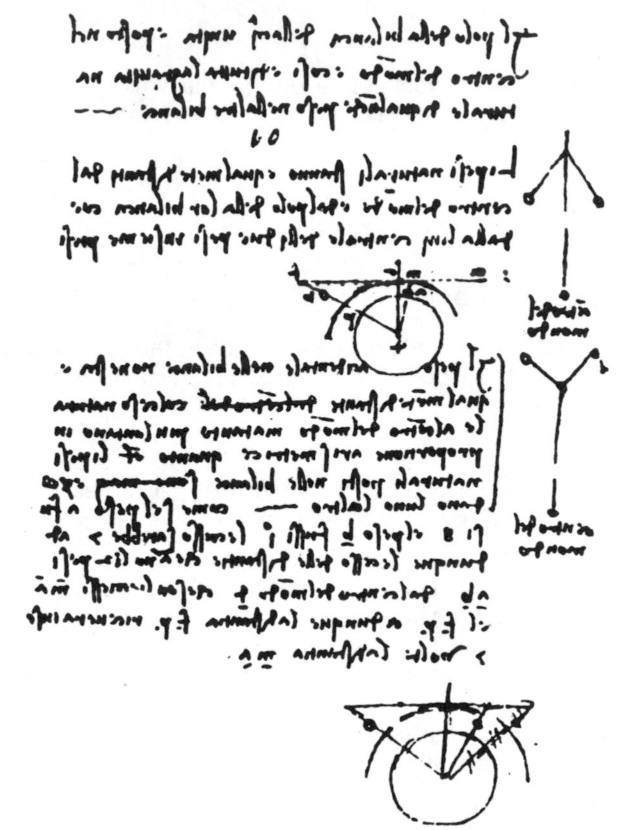

Abb. 5 Eine Seite mit Notizen in Spiegelschrift aus den Skizzenbüchern des Linkshänders Leonardo da Vinci (1452–1519).

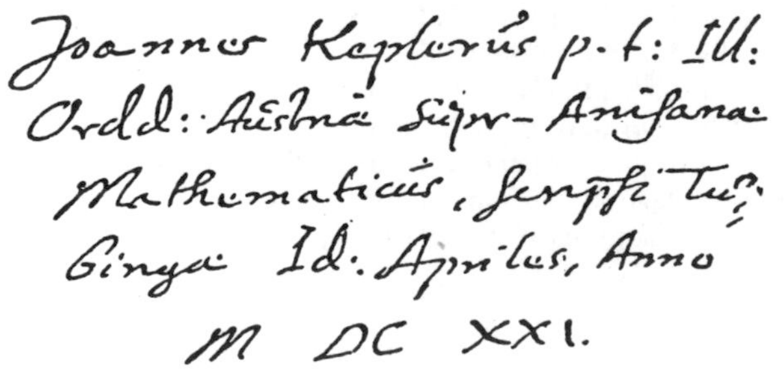
Joannes Keplerus p.t: Ill:
Ordd: Austriae Supr- Anisanae
Mathematicus, Scripsi Tu:
bingae Id: Aprilis, Anno
M DC XXI.

Abb. 6 Lateinische Handschrift des Astronomen Johannes Kepler (1571–1630).

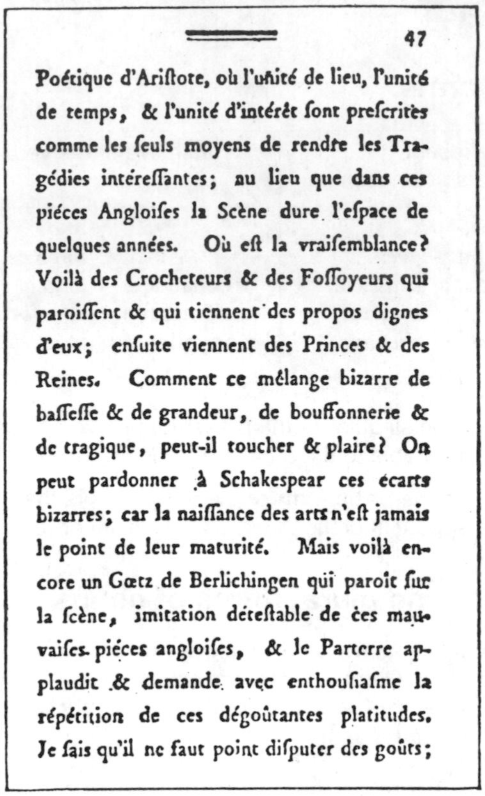
47

Poëtique d'Aristote, où l'unité de lieu, l'unité de temps, & l'unité d'intérêt sont prescrites comme les seuls moyens de rendre les Tragédies intéressantes; au lieu que dans ces piéces Angloises la Scène dure l'espace de quelques années. Où est la vraisemblance? Voilà des Crocheteurs & des Fossoyeurs qui paroissent & qui tiennent des propos dignes d'eux; ensuite viennent des Princes & des Reines. Comment ce mélange bizarre de bassesse & de grandeur, de bouffonnerie & de tragique, peut-il toucher & plaire? On peut pardonner à Schakespear ces écarts bizarres; car la naissance des arts n'est jamais le point de leur maturité. Mais voilà encore un Gœtz de Berlichingen qui paroît sur la scène, imitation détestable de ces mauvaises pièces angloises, & le Parterre applaudit & demande avec enthousiasme la répétition de ces dégoûtantes platitudes. Je sais qu'il ne faut point disputer des goûts;

Abb. 7 Friedrich der Große, „Über die deutsche Literatur" – Seite mit dem Urteil über Goethes Götz. Berlin, 1780.

links	- *left, left-hand*	Seite	- *page; side*
mit	- *with*	Skizze	- *sketch*
Notiz	- *note*	Urteil	- *opinion, judgement*

Friedrich der Große (1712–1786): King of Prussia 1740–1786
Götz (i. e. *Götz von Berlichingen*): play by J. W. v. Goethe 1773

Task:
Listen and follow the text, then read each caption again and say what you have found out from it.

Text: Titles of books and short summaries of their contents.

Quelle: Publishers' catalogues.

Englische Essays aus drei Jahrhunderten
Herausgegeben von A. Schlösser

Die chronologisch aufgebaute und reichkommentierte Anthologie enthält die brillantesten und charakteristischsten Essays englischer Denker vom 17. bis zum 19. Jahrhundert, von Francis Bacon bis Charles Darwin.

aufgebaut	– *built up, structured*
reich	– *rich, copious*
kommentiert	– *annotated* (lit. *commented*)
enthält	– *contains, includes*
brillantesten und charakteristischsten:	superlative forms of *brillant und charakteristisch*

Task 1:
Listen and follow the text; read the text through again and answer the questions.

a Did *A. Schlösser* translate the English essays?
b Who are the essays by?
c Does the book contain commentaries on the essays?
d On the basis of which criteria were the essays selected?
e In what order has the publisher arranged them?

Jeanne Hersch
Karl Jaspers

Eine Einführung in sein Werk

Jeanne Hersch, Professorin für Philosophie in Genf und Schülerin von Karl Jaspers, gibt mit ihrem Buch eine Einführung in Leben und Werk des großen deutschen Philosophen.

Genf	– *Geneva*
ihr	– *her*
Einführung:	Look up the verb einführen in the *Basic Word List;* try to derive the meaning of Einführung from it.
Professorin, Schülerin·	Look up the noun Schüler in the *Basic Word List.* Then read the explanation on the suffix *-in* (see *Suffixes in Nouns*, p. 142).

Task 2:
Listen and follow the text; read the text through again, find out about *einführen*, *Schüler*, and the suffix *-in*, then answer the questions.

a As what is *Karl Jaspers* (1883–1969) described here?
b In what relationship did *Jeanne Hersch* stand to *Jaspers*?
c What is *Jeanne Hersch* today?
d As what may her book be regarded?

Ernst R. Sandvoss
Aristoteles

Schwerpunkte dieses neuen Werkes über den griechischen Philosophen sind der historische Hintergrund der aristotelischen Philosophie sowie seine Sozialphilosophie.

der Schwerpunkt, -e	– *centre, main emphasis, centre of gravity*
sind	– *are*
der Hintergrund	– *background*
sowie	– *as well as*
seine	– *his*

Task 3:
Listen and follow the text; read the text through again, then answer the questions.

a Is this book a new edition of an older work?
b Does it mainly contain texts by *Aristotle* or texts about *Aristotle*?
c Which two topics are especially emphasized?

Walter Gerlach/Martha List
Johannes Kepler
Leben und Werk

Die beiden Autoren zeichnen ein lebendiges Bild der Persönlichkeit und des Lebensweges des genialen Astronomen.

beide	– *both*
die beiden	– *the two*
zeichnen	– *draw, depict*
lebendig:	Adjective, derived from Leben
das Bild	– *image, picture*
der Lebensweg	– *course of one's life, life*
genial	– *ingenious*

Task 4:
Listen and follow the text; read the text through again, then answer the questions.

a As what is *Kepler* (1571–1630) described here?
b Do you suppose that the book is written in a very sober and objective manner?
c After reading this text would you rather ecpect a work on astronomy or a biography?

F. L. Carsten
Faschismus in Österreich

Das Buch des englischen Historikers über den „Austrofaschismus" gründet sich auf eingehende Studien des Autors in deutschen und österreichischen Archiven.

eingehend	– *comprehensive, thorough*
gründet sich:	sich is the reflexive pronoun; it belongs with the verb gründen. Look up the reflexive form of the verb gründen in the *Basic Word List* (gründen vr).

Task 5:
Listen and follow the text; read the text through again, find out about the verb *gründen*, then answer the questions.

a As what is *F. L. Carsten* presented to the reader here?
b What is the English name for *Österreich*?
c How did the author become acquainted with *Austrofaschismus*?

1 Alan J. Taylor
Bismarck
Mensch und Staatsmann

5 Der bekannte Oxforder Historiker zeichnet mit dieser Biographie ein Bismarck-Bild aus eigener Sicht. Psychologisch motivierend und rational interpretierend setzt er sich mit dem Mythos des „Eisernen Kanzlers" auseinander.

bekannt	– *known, well-known*
eigen	– *own, one's own*
die Sicht	– *point of view*
motivierend	– *giving reasons*
interpretierend	– *interpreting*
setzt sich auseinander:	One of the so-called separable verbs; the infinitive is auseinandersetzen; the reflexive pronoun sich belongs with the verb. Look up the reflexive form of the verb auseinandersetzen in the *Basic Word List (auseinandersetzen* vr).
er	– *he*
eisern	– *of iron; like iron*
der Kanzler	– *chancellor*

Task 6:
Listen and follow the text; read the text through again, find out about the verb *auseinandersetzen,* then answer the questions.

a As what is *A. J. Taylor* presented to the reader here?
b Does this book seem to be a strictly objective account of *Bismarck's* life?
c What seems special about this biography?
d What nickname was given to *Bismarck* (1815–1898)?

1 Lothar Gall/Rainer Koch (Hrsg.)
Der europäische Liberalismus im 19. Jahrhundert
Texte zu seiner Entwicklung

5 Diese vier Bände repräsentieren die relevantesten Theorienentwicklungen zu dem Themenkomplex „Liberalismus". Der Historiker Lothar Gall stellt jedem Band ein einführendes Essay voran.

sein	– *its*
die Entwicklung	– *development*
der Band, ⸚	– *volume*
relevant*est:*	Superlative form of the adjective *relevant*
der Themenkomplex:	Compound noun, der Komplex + die Themen
das Thema, Themen	– *subject, topic*
stellt voran:	Present tense singular of voranstellen
voranstellen	– *to put* or *place in front*
jede/jeder/jedes	– *each, every*
einführend	– *introducing, introductory*

Task 7
Listen and follow the text; read the text through again, then answer the questions.

a Are *L. Gall* and *R. Koch* the authors of all the texts in these volumes?

b What are the four volumes mainly about?
c How many introductory essays are there in this work?

1 Eckart Otto
Jerusalem – die Geschichte der Heiligen Stadt
Archäologie, Geschichtswissenschaft und Religionsgeschichte verbinden sich hier zur Darstellung der Stadtentwicklung und ihrer Bedeutung.

5

heilig	– *holy, sacred*
die Stadt, ⸚e	– *town, city*
verbinden sich	– *combine, join*
zur (zu + der)	– *for the*
die Darstellung	– *description, representation*
ihr	– *its*
die Bedeutung	– *importance, meaning*

Task 8:
Listen and follow the text; read the text through again, then answer the questions.

a What other name is given to Jerusalem?
b Which two historical aspects of Jerusalem does the author present in the text?
c Which sciences is his description based upon?

Text: Illustration and caption from a book on the writing, signs and symbols of different peoples.

Quelle: Franz H. Wills, Schrift und Zeichen der Völker, Econ Verlag, Düsseldorf/Wien 1977, S. 75.

Abb. 8 Chinesische Symbole: In der Mitte das Yang-Yin-Zeichen der universalen Harmonie, rundum acht taoistische Diagramme. Die zwölf äußeren Ornamente symbolisieren die kaiserliche Macht und erscheinen zusammen nur auf den Staatsgewändern der Kaiser.

der Kaiser	– *emperor*
die Macht	– *power* (cognate: *might*)
erscheinen	– *appear*
zusammen	– *together*
nur	– *only*
auf	– *on*
das Staatsgewand, ⁻er:	Compound noun das Gewand + der Staat
das Gewand, ⁻er	– *robe, gown*
der Staat	– *state, pomp*

Task:
Listen and follow the text; read the text through again, then answer the questions.

a Which two words tell us which signs we are dealing with here?
b What is the Yang Yin sign a symbol of?
c The three words *Mitte*, *rundum* and *äußeren* describe the position of the individual signs or ornaments. What are the English equivalents?
d What are the ornaments around the outside edge a symbol of? Where do they appear together?

Grammar

1 Verb forms

a In the third person singular of the present tense verbs have the ending -*t* or -*et* (comparable with the ending -*s* in English) and in the third person plural the ending -*en* or -*n*. The same ending also appears in the infinitive.
b The verb *sein* (*to be*) is irregular.
c In the third person singular of some verbs there is a change of vowel: $e \rightarrow i$ and $a \rightarrow \ddot{a}$ (cf. *Verbs, Present Tense*, p. 67).

Present tense, 3rd person		Infinitive	
singular	plural		
a repräsentiert erscheint zeichnet	repräsentieren erscheinen zeichnen	repräsentieren erscheinen zeichnen	*to represent to appear to draw*
b ist	sind	sein	*to be*
c gibt enthält	geben enthalten	geben enthalten	to give to contain

2 Reflexive verbs

In the third person (singular or plural) reflexive verbs are used in conjunction with the pronoun *sich*. Most German reflexive verbs are not reflexive in English (cf. *Reflexive Verbs*, p. 92).

Present tense, 3rd person		Infinitive
singular	plural	
gründet sich verbindet sich	gründen sich verbinden sich	sich gründen sich verbinden

The difference in meaning between the reflexive and the nonreflexive forms of a verb can be very great. Compare:

gründen	*to found*	sich gründen (auf)	*to be based (on)*
verbinden	*to connect*	sich verbinden	*to combine, join*
enthalten	*to contain*	sich enthalten	*to abstain from*

Dictionaries normally indicate reflexive verbs with „vr" or „v. refl.", or they include *sich* with the infinitive. The non-reflexive verbs are mostly indicated by „vt" or „v. tr." and „vi" or „v. itr." (or not especially indicated at all).

3 Verbs with prefixes

Most verbs in German texts are combinations of prefixes and basic verbs. There are verbs with „inseparable" and „separable" prefixes (cf. *Verbs with Prefixes*, pp. 82–85).

a Inseparable prefixes are always attached to the verbs (cf. the English verbs: *get – forget, come – become*).

In this lesson there are three verbs with inseparable prefixes:

| erscheinen | enthalten | sich verbinden |
| *to appear* | *to contain* | *to combine* |

The basic verbs are:

| scheinen | halten | binden |
| *to seem* | *to hold* | *to bind* |

b Separable prefixes appear after the verb in the present and past tenses, usually at the end of the clause (cf. the English verbs: *get – get on, give – give up*).

In this lesson there are two verbs with separable prefixes:

| voranstellen | sich auseinandersetzen (mit etwas) |
| *to put/place in front* | *to have a good look (at something)* |

The basic verbs are:

| stellen | setzen |
| *to put* | *to put, set, place* |

Present tense, 3rd person		Infinitive
singular	plural	
a erscheint enthält verbindet sich	erscheinen enthalten verbinden sich	erscheinen enthalten sich verbinden
b stellt ... voran setzt sich ... auseinander	stellen ... voran setzen sich ... auseinander	voranstellen sich auseinandersetzen

35

4 Superlative form

If an adjective displays the endings -st or -est, then it is a superlative form; it corresponds to the English adjective with -st or the adjective preceded by *most* (cf. *Suffixes*, p. 140, and *Comparison*, p. 59).

brillant	charakteristisch	relevant
brilliant	*characteristic*	*relevant*

die brillantesten und charakteristischsten Essays
the most brilliant and most characteristic essays

die relevantesten Theorieentwicklungen
the most relevant developments of the theory

5 Nouns and proper names

Nouns and proper names are capitalized. All other words, including adjectives derived from nationalities, are written with small initial letters (cf. *Spelling*, p. 15).

das Buch des englischen Historikers
the book of the English historian

in deutschen und österreichischen Archiven
in German and Austrian archives

Essays englischer Denker
essays by English thinkers

über den griechischen Philosophen
on the Greek philosopher

Word formation

1 Nouns derived from nouns

A noun ending in -er often denotes an expert working in a special field. (See *Suffixes in Nouns*, p. 141.)

Task 1:
Find the two related nouns denoting the expert and his field of work in the extracts from the texts and underline them.

a Albert Einstein, deutsch-amerikanischer Physiker
Theoretische Physik auf der Grundlage einer allgemeinen Dynamik
b Johann Wolfgang von Goethe, deutscher Lyriker, Dramatiker, Romanschriftsteller, ...
Goethes Lyrik
c Johann Wolfgang von Goethe, Lyriker, Dramatiker, ... und Wissenschaftler
Goethes Naturwissenschaft
d Bertrand Russell, englischer Philosoph*, Mathematiker und Schriftsteller
Probleme der Philosophie

Task 2:
What are the fields of the following experts?

a der Politiker: die _____ ;

b der Musiker: die _____ ;

c der Mathematiker: die _____

Task 3:
What does the term *Linkshänder* indicate about *Leonardo da Vinci*?

2 Nouns and adjectives derived from verbs

Task 4:
Read through the following extracts from the texts; write the English equivalent of each verb in the space provided, checking it first in the *Basic Word List*; find the words related to the verbs in the extracts and underline them.

a arbeiten – _____
Sozialgeschichte der Arbeit
Geschichte der deutschen Arbeiterbewegung
Goethes naturwissenschaftliche Arbeiten

b denken – _____
Goethe als Denker
Gedanken über Goethe

c wissen – _____
Goethes Naturwissenschaft
J. W. v. Goethe, deutscher Lyriker, Dramatiker, ... und Naturwissenschaftler
Goethes naturwissenschaftliche Arbeiten
Schriften zur Botanik und Wissenschaftslehre

d schreiben – _____
Schriften zur Geologie, Mineralogie und Meteorologie
Bertrand Russell, englischer Philosoph, Mathematiker und Schriftsteller
Lateinische Handschrift des Astronomen Johannes Kepler
Eine Seite mit Notizen in Spiegelschrift aus den Skizzenbüchern des Linkshänders Leonardo da Vinci

3 Nouns with the suffix -in

Nouns with the suffix -in, which is added to nouns designating male beings, denote the corresponding female beings; they are feminine in gender (see *Suffixes*, p. 142).

der Professor, -en *(professor)*	– die Professorin, -nen
der Schüler, – *(disciple/student)*	– die Schülerin, -nen

---

*There are nouns denoting experts which do not take -er, e. g.
der Fotograf – *the photographer* (die Fotografie – *photography*)
der Astronom – *the astronomer* (die Astronomie – *astronomy*).

Text

Text: On the responsibilities of intellect and reason; a quotation from Max Born (German physicist, 1882–1970).

Quelle: Walter R. Fuchs, Knaurs Buch der modernen Mathematik, Droemer Knaur, München/Zürich 1966, S. 271–272.

> **1 Verstand und Vernunft**
> „Der Verstand unterscheidet zwischen möglich und unmöglich. Die Vernunft unterscheidet zwischen sinnvoll und sinnlos. Auch das Mögliche kann sinnlos sein. Es ist z.B. heute
> **5** möglich, alles Leben auf der Erde in kurzer Zeit zu vernichten. Also ist es nicht nur Aufgabe des Verstandes, Grenzen zu erkennen, sondern auch der Vernunft!"

der Verstand	*intellect*	der Sinn	*sense, point*
die Vernunft	*reason*	sinnvoll	*sensible, useful*
kann . . . sein	*can be . . .*	unterscheiden	*to distinguish*
möglich	*possible*	vernichten	*to annihilate*

Task 1:
Look at the words given and locate them in the text above, then look up the other words in the *Basic Word List* and write down their meanings.

also _____

auch _____

die Aufgabe _____

die Erde _____

erkennen _____

die Grenze _____

heute _____

kurz _____

das Leben _____

nicht nur _____

sondern auch _____

die Zeit _____

z.B. = zum Beispiel _____

Task 2:
Listen and follow the text, then read it again to yourself.

Task 3:
Find the two pairs of antonyms in the text and write them down.

_____   _____

_____   _____

Task 4:
Find the German equivalents in the text and write them down.

Even the possible can be senseless.

_____

It is possible to destroy every living thing on earth.

_____

Therefore it is the responsibility of reason . . .

_____

. . . to recognize boundaries.

_____

Task 5:
Answer the questions.
a Where does *Max Born* draw the limits of human possibility?
b What is, for him, the superior yardstick: intellect or reason?
c Would you describe this position as purely scientific?

Task 6:
Fill in the missing words (reconstruction of the text).

Der Verstand unterscheidet zwischen möglich und _____. Die Vernunft _____ zwischen sinnvoll und _____. Auch das Mögliche kann sinn_____ sein. Es ist z.B. heute _____, alles _____ auf der Erde in kurzer _____ zu vernichten. _____ ist es nicht nur Aufgabe des Verstandes, _____ zu erkennen, _____ auch der Vernunft.

Word formation

An adjective like *möglich* is made negative with the prefix *un-*.
The adjective suffix *-voll* corresponds to the English suffix *-ful*.
The adjective suffix *-los* corresponds to the English suffix *-less*.

7

Text: Titles of books and short summaries of their contents.

Quelle: Publishers' catalogues.

---

1 H. Gastager/S. Gastager (Hg.)
Hilfe in Krisen
Der Mensch kann in psychische, körperliche oder soziale Krisen geraten und zusammenbrechen. Oft ist dann nicht der „Experte" zur Stelle, sondern der „Nächste" muß Krisenhilfe leisten. Für Theologen, Mediziner, Psychologen, Pädagogen, Juristen und Sozialarbeiter bietet dieses Buch viele wertvolle Informationen.

5

Task 1:
Listen and follow the text, then write down the probable meanings of the following words.

die Hilfe, -n _____

die Krise, -n _____

der Mensch, -en _____

oft _____

dann _____

der Experte, -n _____

kann _____

muß _____

Task 2:
Read the text again with the aid of the words listed below and then answer the questions.

körperlich	*physical*
geraten (in)	*to get (into)*
zusammenbrechen	*to break down*
zur Stelle	*at hand, on the spot*
sondern	*but*
der Nächste	*the neighbour* (lit: *the next one*)
Hilfe leisten	*to lend support, to give help*
bieten	*to offer*
viele	*many*
wertvoll	*valuable* (lit: *worth-ful*)

a Which human crises are mentioned?
b Who is responsible for supplying aid in such crises?
c To whom is this book especially recommended?

---

1 Alan Palmer
Bismarck
Eine Biographie

In dieser Biographie, die den neuesten Stand der Forschung berücksichtigt, schildert der Autor Bismarcks privates und öffentliches Leben mit neuen Details.

5

Task 3:
Listen and follow the text, then read it again to yourself. Then write the English equivalents under the German words. Finally discuss the solutions and answer the question at the end.

In dieser Biographie,   die den neuesten

_____, *which* _____

Stand der	Forschung berücsichtigt	schildert
state of (developments in)	*research takes into account,*	*describes*

der Autor	Bismarcks	privates
_____	_____	_____

und öffentliches Leben mit neuen Details

___ *public* _____

How is this Bismarck biography different from those which appeared earlier?

---

1 Peter Zudeick
Alternative Schulen
Immer mehr Schüler, Eltern und Lehrer, die mit dem staatlichen Schulwesen unzufrieden sind, suchen heute nach Alternativen, über die dieser Band informiert.

5

Task 4:
Listen and follow the text, then read it again to yourself. Then write the German equivalents under the English expressions. Finally discuss the solutions and answer the three questions at the end.

a *alternatives about which this volume informs us*

_____

b *with the state school system*

_____

c *parents and teachers are today looking for alternatives*

_____

d *more and more pupils*

_____

e *teachers who are dissatisfied*

_____

f What do a lot of parents think of the state school system?
g How do they react to it?
h Could this book be regarded as a sort of „advisor"? Why (not)?

1 Hans Hörmann
   ## Einführung in die Psycholinguistik
   Das Buch stellt die Probleme dar, die sich ergeben, wenn man die Verwendung von Sprache wissenschaftlich
5 beschreiben und erklären will.

Task 5:
Listen and follow the text, then read it again to yourself. Read the text with the aid of the words listed below and then answer the questions.

stellt . . . dar	*shows, portrays*
sich ergeben	*arise, result*
wenn	*when, if*
man	*one, they, we, you*
die Verwendung	*use, employment*
beschreiben	*to describe*
erklären	*to explain*
will	*wants to*

a Is the author, judging by the title of his book, dealing with a specialist area of linguistics?
b Which problems does the author present to the reader?
c What is, according to this short summary of the contents, the task of psycholinguistics?

Text: Illustration and caption from a book on the writing, signs and symbols of different peoples.

Quelle: Franz H. Wills, Schrift und Zeichen der Völker, Econ Verlag, Düsseldorf/Wien 1977, S. 148.

Abb. 9 Vorgeschichtliche Jagdszenen von einem Felsen in der nordarabischen Wüste. Während die Jäger oben auf Pferden reiten, sitzt der Straußenjäger auf einem zweihöckrigen Kamel.

Task 1:
Listen and follow the text, then read it again to yourself. Write the German passages from the text next to the English equivalents. Discuss the solutions.

_____ *the ostrich hunter*

_____ *prehistoric hunting scenes*

_____ *the hunters at the top*

_____ *on horses*

_____ *on a two-humped camel*

_____ *in the desert*

_____ *from a rock*

während *while, whereas*

Task 2:
Answer the questions.

a What kind of words do you think *reiten* and *sitzt* are? What do they mean?

   Die Jäger reiten

_____

   Der Straußenjäger sitzt

_____

b Are all of the figures in the illustration mentioned in the text?

39

7

Text: This illustration and text are from a book on psychology and are taken from the part dealing with perception; the text is concerned with two generally familiar examples of optical illusions.

Quelle: Charlotte Bühler, Psychologie im Leben unserer Zeit, Droemer Knaur Verlag, München/Zürich 1962, zit. nach Knaur Taschenbuch, Band 269. München/Zürich 1972, S. 39.

Optische Täuschungen

1 . . . Unter den optischen Täuschungen ist besonders bekannt die sogenannte Müller-Lyersche Täuschung, die als eines der zuerst entdeckten klassischen Beispiele gelten kann.

5 Die beiden Linien sind tatsächlich gleich lang, obwohl infolge der Anordnung der Pfeile die eine wesentlich länger erscheint.

Im zweiten Beispiel erscheint der innere Kreis viel größer, wenn er im Mittelpunkt kleiner Kreise steht, als wenn größere 10 ihn umgeben. Tatsächlich ist jedoch der innere Kreis beide Male gleich groß.

Abb. 10 Zwei klassische Beispiele optischer Täuschung: Die linke, länger wirkende Strecke ist genauso lang wie die rechte, und der von kleineren Kreisen umgebene innere Kreis ist ebenso groß wie der scheinbar kleinere Kreis, der von fünf großen Kreisen eingeschlossen ist.

Task 1:
Look at the lines and circles in the illustration and consider the following questions.
a Which of the horizontal segments of the line appears to be the longer?
b Which of the two inner circles seems to be the larger?
c What do we discover if we measure the lines and circles?

Task 2:
Listen and follow the text. Find the German equivalents in the text and underline them.

a *Both lines are, in fact, equally long.*
b *One appears considerably longer.*
c *The inner circle appears much bigger if it is at the centre of small circles.*
d *In actual fact, the inner circle is equally large in both cases.*

Task 3:
Find the German equivalents in the text and enter them in the gaps provided.

a *equally long* _____

b *considerably longer* _____

c *much bigger* _____

d *equally large* _____

e *just as long as* _____

f *just as large as* _____

Task 4:
Try to guess the meaning of *obwohl* and *als* by supplying appropriate words in the English context.

a Die beiden Linien sind tatsächlich gleich lang, obwohl die eine wesentlich länger erscheint.

Both lines are, in fact, equally long _____ *one appears to be considerably longer.*

b Der innere Kreis erscheint viel größer, wenn er im Mittelpunkt kleiner Kreise steht, als wenn größere ihn umgeben.

The inner circle appears much bigger if it is at the centre of

small circles, _____ *if surrounded by bigger ones* (lit: *if bigger ones surround it*).

Task 5:
Find the German equivalents in the text and underline them.

a *of all optical illusions* (lit. *among the . . .*)
b *one of the first classic examples to be discovered*
c *in the second example*
d *two classic examples of optical illusion*
e *the left-hand segment of the line*
f *the apparently smaller circle*

Task 6:
Find the two antonyms in the text and enter them in the gaps provided.

a die linke Strecke – die _____ Strecke

b größere Kreise – der _____ Kreis

Anordnung	*arrangement*
bekannt	*well known*
eingeschlossen	*surrounded* (lit. *enclosed*)
kann gelten als	*can be regarded as*
infolge	*as a result of*
jedoch	*however*
Pfeil, -e	*arrow*
sogenannt	*so-called*

Task 7:
Find three adverbs which modify adjectives in the text and enter them in the gaps provided.

a *especially well known* – _____ bekannt;

b *considerably longer* – _____ länger;

c *much bigger* – _____ größer

Task 8:
Find two synonymous expressions in the text and write them underneath.

a der innere Kreis, wenn er im Mittelpunkt kleiner Kreise steht:

der _____

b (der innere Kreis), wenn größere ihn umgeben:

der Kreis, der _____

Text: Illustration with caption from a book on cultural anthropology taken from a section on computer-art in a chapter on aesthetics.

Quelle: H.-G. Gadamer/P. Vogler (Hrsg.), Neu Anthropologie, Bd. 4: Kulturanthropologie, Georg Thieme Verlag Stuttgart 1973. Abdruck mit freundlicher Genehmigung der Boeing Company, Düsseldorf.

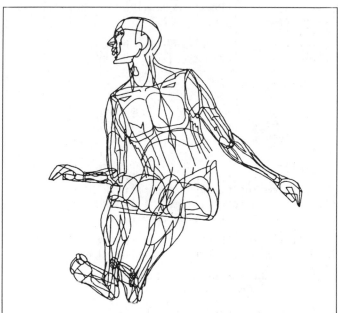

Abb. 11 Mit einem Computer generierte ergonomische Studie eines Piloten (Boeing Company).

Task 1:
Listen and follow the text; write the English expressions under the German ones; compare the word order in both languages.

Mit	einem	Computer	generierte
_____	_____	_____	_____

ergonomische	Studie	eines
_____	_____	_____

Piloten

_____

Task 2:
Answer the questions.

a Whom or what does the illustration depict?
b How did it come about?
c What would the caption be in correct English?

Grammar

1 Modal auxiliaries

In the third person singular of the present modal verbs have no ending (other verbs have the ending -t or -et).
Unlike in Englisch German modal verbs also have an infinitive form (cf. *Modal Auxiliaries*, p. 77).

Present tense, 3rd person		Infinitive	
singular	plural		
kann	können	können	*(to be able to)*
muß	müssen	müssen	*(to have to)*
will	wollen	wollen	*(to want to)*

Modal verbs almost always appear with a further verb in the infinitive form. Unlike in English the verb in the infinitive form normally comes at the end of a clause.

Der Mensch *kann* in Krisen *geraten* und *zusammenbrechen*.
The human being can get *into crises and* break down.

. . . sondern der Nächste *muß* Krisenhilfe *leisten*.
. . . *but the neighbour* must lend *support in a crisis*.

Auch das Mögliche *kann* sinnlos *sein*.
Even the possible can be *without meaning*.

2 Infinitive with *zu*

While the simple infinitive is used with modal verbs, in almost all other cases the infinitive is used with the preposition *zu*. This infinitive form also usually comes at the end of a clause (cf. *Infinitive: Use*, p. 86).

Es ist heute möglich, alles Leben auf der Erde *zu vernichten*.
Today it is possible to destroy *every living thing on earth*.

Also ist es nicht nur Aufgabe des Verstandes, Grenzen *zu erkennen*, . . .
Therefore it is not only the responsibility of intellect to recognize boundaries, . . .

3 Word order (verbs)

While German word order is generally freer than in English the position of the verb is strictly determined (cf. *Word Order (Verbs)*, p. 100).
In a main clause the verb occupies second place (except in certain questions and requests).

Der Verstand *unterscheidet* zwischen möglich und unmöglich.
Intellect distinguishes *between possible and impossible*.

In diesem Werk *behandelt* Grimm das religiöse Leben . . .
In this work Grimm deals with *the religious life* . . .

Nach Heraklit *ist* der Krieg der Vater aller Dinge.
According to Heraclitus war is *the father of all things*.

In a subordinate clause the verb always occupies final position. Subordinate clauses, or dependent clauses, cannot normally appear on their own in a text. They include relative clauses and clauses which are introduced by particular words, so-called conjunctions, e.g. *wenn (if/when)*, *während (while/whereas)*, *obwohl (although)*, (cf. *A List of Common Conjunctions*, p. 105).

Relative clauses:

In dieser Biographie, *die* den neuesten Stand der Forschung *berücksichtigt*, . . .
In this biography, which takes into account *the latest developments in research*, . . .

. . . Eltern und Lehrer, *die* mit dem staatlichen Schulwesen unzufrieden *sind*, . . .
. . . *parents and teachers*, who are *dissatisfied with the state school system* . . .

. . . Alternativen, *über die* dieser Band *informiert*.
. . . *alternatives*, about which *this volume informs us*.

. . . der scheinbar kleinere Kreis, *der* von fünf großen Kreisen eingeschlossen *ist*.
. . . *the apparently smaller circle* which is *surrounded by five large circles*.

Subordinate clauses introduced by conjunctions:

Während die Jäger . . . auf Pferden *reiten*, . . .
While *the hunters* ride *on horses*, . . .

. . . Probleme, die sich ergeben, *wenn* man die Verwendung von Sprache . . . erklären *will*.
. . . *problems which occur* when *one* wishes *to explain the use of language*.

Im zweiten Beispiel erscheint der innere Kreis viel größer, *wenn* er im Mittelpunkt kleinerer Kreise *steht*, als *wenn* größere ihn *umgeben*.
In the second example the inner circle appears to be much bigger when *it is at the centre of smaller circles than* when *it is surrounded by larger ones*.

Die beiden Linien sind tatsächlich gleich lang, *obwohl* die eine wesentlich länger *erscheint*.
Both lines are in fact equally long, although *one* appears to be *substantially longer*.

4 Adjectives before nouns

Adjectives and participles modifying a noun come before the noun. They have endings (-e, -em, -en, -er or -es):

das *religiöse* Leben der *germanischen* Völker
the religious *life of the* Germanic *peoples*

Leben und Werk des *großen deutschen* Philosophen
life and work of the great German *philosopher*

die *sogenannte Müller-Lyersche* Täuschung
the so-called Müller-Lyer *illusion*

5 Adverbs before adjectives

When an adjective or a participle is modified by an adverb the adverb comes before the adjective or participle. The adverb has no ending (cf. *Adjectives and Adverbs*, p. 58).

die *chronologisch* aufgebaute Anthologie
the chronologically *constructed anthology*

der *scheinbar* kleinere Kreis
the apparently *smaller circle*

6 Word order (extended adjectives)

Adjectives or participles occurring in front of a noun are sometimes modified by further words. These additional expressions appear before the adjective or participle. In English such extended modifiers normally occur after the noun (cf. *Word Order (Adjectives)*, p. 111).

der von kleineren Kreisen umgebene innere Kreis
(literally: *the by-smaller-circles-surrounded inner circle*)
the inner circle surrounded by smaller ones

die linke, länger wirkende Seite
(literally: *the left-hand longer-appearing line*)
the left-hand line which appears longer

eines der zuerst entdeckten klassischen Beispiele
(literally: *one of the first-discovered classic examples*)
one of the first classic examples to be discovered

mit einem Computer generierte ergonomische Studie eines Piloten
(literally: *with-a-computer-generated ergonomic study of a pilot*)
ergonomic study of a pilot generated by a computer

7 *so – wie* in comparisons

If an adjective is preceded by *so* and followed by *wie*, a comparison is intended.

Der innere Kreis ist *ebenso* groß *wie* der scheinbar kleinere Kreis, . . .
The inner circle is just as *large* as *the apparently smaller circle*, . . .

Die linke Strecke ist *genauso* lang *wie* die rechte . . .
The left-hand line is just as *long* as *the right-hand one* . . .

8 Comparative form

To form the comparative the ending *-er* is added to the basic form of the adjective. This corresponds to the English ending *-er* or *more* in front of the adjective. In short words the root of the adjective is sometimes *umlaut*ed (cf. *Comparison*, p. 59).

klein   klein*er*   groß   größ*er*   lang   läng*er*
*small   small*er   *big, large big*ger*, larg*er   *long   long*er

Die beiden Linien sind gleich lang, obwohl die eine *länger* erscheint.
Both lines are equally long although one appears to be longer.

der scheinbar *kleinere* Kreis
the apparently smaller *circle*

8

Text

Text: Titles of books and short summaries of their contents.

Quelle: Publishers' catalogues.

1 Peter Lösche

Anarchismus

Historiker, Politologen und Soziologen haben den Anarchismus, seine sozialen Grundlagen und seine prominentesten
5 Vertreter analysiert und dargestellt. Ein Überblick über die Forschungsergebnisse ist nicht nur von wissenschaftlichem, sondern auch von aktuellem Interesse.

aktuell	– *topical, relevant, present*
das Ergebnis, -se	– *result, outcome*
die Forschung, -en	– *research*
nicht nur . . ., sondern auch . . .	– *not only . . ., but also . . .*
der Überblick	– *overview, survey, synopsis*

Task 1:
Listen and follow the text, then find the German equivalents in the text and write them down.

a *its most prominent advocates*

_____

b *its social basis*

_____

c *of topical interest*

_____

d *historians have analysed and described anarchism*

_____

Task 2:
Answer the questions.

a Who has described the basic prinicples and chief representatives of anarchism?
b What does the book offer the reader?
c Which two qualities make this book interesting?

1 Dieter E. Zimmer

Der Mythos der Gleichheit

Gibt es einen angeborenen Unterschied zwischen Männern und Frauen, zwischen den Rassen? Zimmer hat mit dieser
5 Präsentation neuester biologischer Forschungsergebnisse eine brisante Diskussion in Gang gesetzt.

Task 3:
Consult the *Basic Word List* on

der Gang: in Gang setzen _____

die Gleichheit _____

der Unterschied _____

Task 4:
Listen and follow the text, then find the German equivalents in the text and write them down.

a *difference between the races*

_____

b *Is there an innate difference . . .?*

_____

c *an explosive discussion*

_____

d *between men and women*

_____

Task 5:
Answer the questions.

a Which questions are the main theme of the book?
b What is the author presenting?
c What has apparently happened as a result of the publication of this book?
d Does the author consider innate differences to be at least possible? (Note the title of his book.)

Karl Hermann Schelkle 1

Paulus

Der Apostel Paulus ist durch seine Briefe Lehrer der Kirche. Ihre großen Stunden (Augustinus, Reformation) sind Stunden des Paulus gewesen. Als Apostel und Missionar hat er das 5 christliche Abendland mitbegründet. Er ist also bis heute gegenwärtig.

Task 6:
Listen and follow the text. Underline all the words in the text which you already know or can guess. Which of these words fit in with the title of the book?

Task 7:
Read the text which follows once again. In order to help you the English translations of some of the words are given beneath them.

Der Apostel Paulus ist durch   seine BriefeLehrer der
         through/by   *letters teacher*

Kirche. Ihre großen Stunden (Augustinus, Reformation) sind
  Its   *hours*   *have*

Stunden des Paulus gewesen. Als Apostel und Missionar hat er
            been   *he*
das christliche Abendland   mitbegründet.
      Occident ("evening-land") "co-founded"/"co-
         Er ist also   bis   heute gegenwärtig.
established"   *therefore until today present.*

Task 8:
Answer the questions.

a   What is *Paul* described as here?
b   What role do *Paul*'s letters play?
c   What occasions have been described as "Hours of St. Paul"?
d   What did the apostle and missionary *Paul* achieve?
e   Does *Paul* still have any significance for us today?

---

1 | Milko Kelemen
Klanglabyrinthe
Reflexionen eines Komponisten über die Neue Musik
Mit einem Interview von Joachim Kaiser

5 | Was ist Neue Musik? Warum ist die Neue Musik so schwer zu verstehen? Hat die Neue Musik eine Zukunft? Ein zeitgenössischer Komponist, Dirigent, Organisator der Zagreber Biennale für moderne Musik gibt Auskunft.

die Auskunft, ⸚e	– *information*
der Dirigent, -en	– *conductor*
der Klang, ⸚e	– *sound, tone*
der Komponist, -en	– *composer*
schwer	– *difficult*
verstehen	– *to understand*
warum	– *why*
zeitgenössisch	– *contemporary*
die Zukunft	– *future*
Zagreber Biennale:	– *In Zagreb (Yugoslavia) there is a music festival every two years.*

Task 9:
Listen and follow the text. Read the text once again and answer the following questions.

a   Which three questions does the author deal with?
b   What do we learn about Kelemen in the text?
c   What kind of interview is reproduced in the book?

Text: Some questions about the origin of language from a chapter on the beginnings of comparative linguistics.

Quelle: Hans Joachim Störig, Kleine Weltgeschichte der Wissenschaft, Bd. 2, Verlag W. Kohlhammer, Stuttgart 1954. © Hans Joachim Störig.

Was ist Sprache?   1

Was ist Sprache? Wie kommt es, daß es verschiedene Sprachen gibt? Hängen sie untereinander zusammen, und wie? Wie ist die Sprache, wie sind die Sprachen entstanden? Wie   5
sind die Wörter entstanden? Wie kommt es, daß eine bestimmte Sache in einer bestimmten Sprache so und nicht anders benannt wird? Ist das reine Willkür, Übereinkunft, oder besteht eine innere Beziehung zwischen den Gegenständen und ihren Namen?
. . .

Task 1:
Listen and follow the text; then read the text again to yourself and underline the word occurring most frequently.

Task 2:
Find the German equivalents in the text and write them in; then read the text once more to yourself.

_____	*language*
_____	*different languages*
_____	*in a particular language*
_____	*words*
_____	*names*
_____	*a particular thing*
_____	*an inner relationship*
_____	*between objects and*
_____	*their names*

Task 3:
Answer the questions:

a   What do all of the sentences have in common formally?
b   What is the text about?

> Was ist Sprache? Wie kommt es, daß es verschiedene Sprachen gibt? Hängen sie untereinander zusammen, und wie? Wie ist die Sprache, wie sind die Sprachen entstanden? Wie
> 5 sind die Wörter entstanden? Wie kommt es, daß eine bestimmte Sache in einer bestimmten Sprache so und nicht anders benannt wird? Ist das reine Willkür, Übereinkunft, oder besteht eine innere Beziehung zwischen den Gegenständen und ihren Namen?
> . . .

Task 4:
Find the German equivalents in the text and write them on the right. Dots indicate that certain words will have to be omitted; brackets indicate that the actual text will have to be expanded by words to be found in the text.

a *How did language . . . originate?*

b *How did languages originate?*

c *How did words originate?*

d *How is it that there are different languages?*

e *How is it that a certain thing . . . is called this and not something else?*

f *Is this sheer arbitrariness (or) convention?*

g *Does an inner relationship exist between objects and their names?*

h *Are (languages) interrelated?*

i *And how (are languages interrelated)?*

Grammar

1 Past participle

Regular verbs have a past participle ending in *-t* or *-et*, irregular verbs in *-en*. (This may be compared with the English *-ed* as in *asked* and *-en* as in *written*). A further feature of the past participle is the syllable *ge-*. With simple verbs it occurs at the beginning of the word as a prefix and in verbs with separable prefixes between the prefix and the stem of the verb. This syllable *ge-* does not appear in verbs which end in *-ieren* and in verbs with an inseparable prefix (cf. *Past Participle*, p. 88).

setzen	gesetzt	analysieren	analysiert
to set	*set*	*to analyse*	*analysed*
sein	gewesen	entstehen	entstanden
to be	*been*	*to originate*	*originated*
darstellen	dargestellt	(from: stehen	gestanden)
to describe	*described*	*stand*	*stood*
(from: stellen	gestellt)		
to put	*put*		

2 Perfect tense

The perfect is a verb form with two parts. It consists of an auxiliary verb, mostly *haben (to have)*, in some verbs *sein (to be)* in combination with the past participle of the verb. The participle is almost always at the end of the clause (cf. *Perfect Tenses*, p. 69):

Zimmer *hat . . .* eine brisante Diskussion in Gang *gesetzt.*
Zimmer has set *an explosive discussion going . . .*

Historiker . . . *haben* den Anarchismus *analysiert* und *dargestellt.*
Historians . . . have analysed *and* described *anarchism.*

Ihre großen Stunden *sind* Stunden des Paulus *gewesen*
Its great hours were *hours of St. Paul.*

Wie *ist* die Sprache, *sind* die Sprachen *entstanden?*
How did *language,* did *languages originate?*

3 Questions

The texts in this chapter exemplify both kinds of questions: questions beginning with a verb, and questions beginning with an interrogative. Interrogatives are easy to recognize in German: they begin with the letter *W*:

Hat die Neue Musik eine Zukunft?
Does *Modern Music* have *a future?*

Besteht eine innere Beziehung zwischen den Gegenständen und ihren Namen?
Does *an inner relationship* exist *between objects and their names?*

Warum ist die Neue Musik so schwer zu verstehen?
Why *is Modern Music so difficult to understand?*

Was ist Sprache?
What *is language?*

Wie sind die Wörter entstanden?
How *did words originate?*

Word formation

1 Suffix *-er*

Geographical names to which the ending *-er* has been added can appear in front of nouns as adjectives. They then designate the location or the place of origin of persons or objects (cf. *Suffixes in Adjectives, -er,* p. 136):

der bekannte Oxford*er* Historiker
the well-known Oxford historian

Organisator der Zagreb*er* Biennale
organizer of the Zagreb biennial festival

2 Suffix *-sch*

Personal names to which the suffix *-sch* (and the adjectival endings *-e/-em/-en/-er/-es*) have been added can appear in front of nouns as adjectives (cf. *Suffixes in Adjectives, -sch,* p. 139):

die sogenannte Müller-Lyer*sch*e Täuschung
the so-called Müller-Lyer illusion

3 Basic verb *stehen* and three derivatives

In this chapter there are three derivatives of the verb *stehen (to stand)* formed with inseparable prefixes:

be*stehen* – ent*stehen* – ver*stehen*
to exist – to originate – to understand

wenn er im Mittelpunkt kleiner Kreise *steht.*
if it is at the centre of small circles.

oder *besteht* eine innere Beziehung . . .?
or does an internal relationship exist . . .?

Wie *ist* die Sprache *entstanden?*
How did language originate?

Warum ist die Neue Musik so schwer zu *verstehen?*
Why is Modern Music so difficult to understand?

4 Verbal expression *es gibt*

The form *es gibt* is an impersonal form of the verb *geben (to give),* which often appears in texts. This form always occurs in the singular; the subject is *es (it).* The English equivalents are *there is* or *there are:*

Gibt es einen angeborenen Unterschied zwischen Männern und Frauen?
Is there *an innate difference between men and women?*

Wie kommt es, daß *es* verschiedene Sprachen *gibt?*
How is it that there are *different languages?*

5 Conjunction *daß*

The word *daß* introduces subordinate clauses (dependent clauses). The verb appears at the end of the clause (cf. *List of Common Conjunctions,* p. 106).

Wie kommt es, *daß* es verschiedene Sprachen *gibt?*
How is it that *there* are *different languages?*

4 Two compounds

The separable verb *zusammenhängen (to be joined, to be connected)* consists of the verb *hängen (to hang)* and *zusammen (together)* and means translated literally: *to hang together.*
The adverb *untereinander* is a compound of *unter (under, among)* and *einander (one another, each other).*

Hängen sie (die Sprachen) untereinander zusammen?
(lit.: "*Hang they* (the languages) *among one another together?*")

Admittedly this is not English, but a word for word translation of this sort can help a reader to grasp the sense of a German sentence more precisely than would be the case with a correct translation: "*Are they interrelated?*"

5 Deceptive words

As a rule words which look similar in English and German and mostly have the same basic meaning are a great help in reading the foreign language. There is unfortunately, however, a small number of words which can mislead the reader because they look similar in both languages but have different meanings. It is useful to take a closer look at such "false friends" if misunderstandings are to be avoided (see *Deceptive Words,* p. 190).

aktuell – *topical, relevant, current:* (rarely: *actual*)

Ein Überblick ist von aktuellem Interesse.
A survey is of topical interest.

also – *therefore, so, that is:* (never: *also!*)

Als Apostel und Missionar hat er das christliche Abendland mitbegründet. Er ist also bis heute gegenwärtig.
As an apostle and missionary he was one of the founders of the Christian Occident. Therefore he is present to this day.

Text

Text: The text is from a work by two German biologists. In it they present a general theory to account for the social behaviour of all living beings. The text which follows is the beginning of the chapter on *Verständigung* (*communication*).

Quelle: Wolfgang Wickler/Uta Seibt, Das Prinzip Eigennutz, Ursachen und Konsequenzen sozialen Verhaltens, © Hoffmann und Campe Verlag, Hamburg 1977.

Verständigung

1 Jede Form sozialen Lebens basiert auf Verständigung. Verständigung aber kostet Zeit, Energie und Risiko. Hier spielen Ökonomie-Gesichtspunkte deshalb eine besonders deutliche
5 Rolle. Ein Verständigungs-System braucht Sender und Empfänger sowie Signale oder Nachrichten, die (definitionsgemäß) vom Sender zum Empfänger gehen und diese Strecke in einem Übertragungs- oder Nachrichtenkanal zurücklegen. Wir besprechen deshalb nacheinander das Empfangen, Über-
10 tragen und Senden von Signalen.
Zur Verständigung untereinander benutzen Tiere alle Arten von Signalen, für deren Empfang sie Sinnesorgane haben, z.B. optische, akustische, chemische, taktile, elektrische; man spricht von verschiedenen Modalitäten. Für bestimmte
15 Nachrichten lassen sich mehrere dieser Sinnesreize kombinieren, sie kommen auf verschiedenen Kanälen gleichzeitig beim Empfänger an. Jede Modalität aber hat andere Vor- und Nachteile. Optische und chemische Signale etwa kann man als Marken irgendwo anbringen und hinterlassen, akustische
20 nicht. Akustische und chemische Signale gehen „um die Ecke", optische nicht.

Task 1:
Listen and follow the text, then answer the following questions.

a What kind of signals are mentioned in the text?
b What role is played by all these signals?

Task 2:
Find the German equivalents in the text and underline them. Discuss the solutions.

a *time, energy and risk*
b *economic considerations play a role*
c *transmitters and receivers as well as signals or information*
d *from transmitter to receiver*
e *by means of a transmission or information channel*
f *the reception and transmission of signals*
g *all kinds of signals*
h *sense organs*
i *of various procedures*
j *for certain kinds of information*
k *several of these sense stimuli*
l *by way of different channels*
m *its own advantages and disadvantages* (literally: *„other advantages…"*)
n *optical signals can be deposited in the form of marks* (literally: *„one can fasten optical signals as marks"*)
o *chemical signals go „round corners"*

Task 3:
Put a circle round each verb in the text, then discuss the solutions.

Task 4:
After you have gained a rough idea of what the text is about read it through several times in order to get a better idea of its meaning. Concentrate on the general content rather than on individual features of the text. You already know some of the words; more of them you can guess, and the basic meaning of yet other words is given in the text.

Jede Form sozialen Lebens basiert auf Verständigung. Ver- 1
every   *is based on*

ständigung aber   kostet Zeit, Energie und Risiko. Hier
     but/however

spielen Ökonomie-Gesichtspunkte deshalb   eine besonders
     therefore   *particularly*

deutliche Rolle. Ein Verständigungssystem braucht   Sen-
significant   *needs/requires*

der und Empfänger sowie   Signale oder Nachrichten,   die 5
     as well as   *which*

(definitionsgemäß) vom Sender zum Empfänger gehen und diese
by definition

Strecke in einem Übertragungs- und Nachrichtenkanal zurück-
distance   *cover*

legen. Wir besprechen deshalb nacheinander   das Empfan-
     discuss   *therefore one after the other*

gen, Übertragen und Senden von Signalen. Zur   Verständi-
     for the

gung untereinander   benutzen Tiere   alle Arten von Si- 10
among one another use/employ animals

gnalen, für deren   Empfang sie Sinnesorgane haben,
     whose/of which

z.B. optische, akustische, chemische, taktile, elektrische; man
     one

spricht von verschiedenen Modalitäten. Für bestimmte Nachrich-
speaks

ten lassen sich mehrere dieser Sinnesreize kombinieren, sie
can be

kommen auf verschiedenen Kanälen gleichzeitig   beim 15
arrive   *at the same time*   *at the*

Empfänger an. Jede Modalität aber   hat andere
     every   *but/however*   *other/different*

Vor- und Nachteile. Optische und chemische Signale etwa
     for instance

kann man als Marken irgendwo   anbringen und hinterlassen,
   one   *somewhere fix/fasten*   *leave (behind)*

akustische nicht. Akustische und chemische Signale gehen „um

die Ecke", optische nicht.

Task 5:
Find the German equivalents in the text and write them down.
Note that certain words have been omitted.

a *Communication involves time and energy.*

b *Economic considerations here play a significant role.*

c *A system of communication requires transmitters as well as signals.*

d *We speak of various procedures.*

e *They arrive at the receiver at the same time.*

f *Every procedure has its own advantages.*

Task 6:
Answer the questions relying exclusively on information supplied in the text.

a Are there also certain economic aspects to communication?
b What constitutes a complete system of communication?
c What kinds of signals are used by animals in order to communicate with one another?
d What are the respective advantages and disadvantages of optical, acoustic and chemical signals?

Task 7:
Compare the following statements with the text and select one of the following alternatives:

a This statement appears as such in the text or in other words. Indicate the relevant part of the text.
b This statement does not appear in the text and/or it contradicts the text. What does the text actually have to say on this point?

1 Social life would not be possible without communication.
2 Since communication requires energy, it should be conducted as economically as possible.
3 A communications-system can also function without a transmission or information channel.
4 Even animals which cannot receive chemical signals sometimes employ them.
5 If a piece of information is to be unambiguous, various signals are combined with one another.
6 If a piece of information consists of combined sensory stimuli, these are all received at the same time by the receiver.
7 In certain circumstances even optical signals can go round corners.

Grammar

1 Pronoun *man*

The indefinite pronoun *man* is always the subject of the clause. It usually corresponds to the English *one* or *we*. It often occurs where there would be a „passive construction" in English (cf. *Pronouns*, p. 35).

Man spricht von verschiedenen Modalitäten.
We speak of various procedures.

Optische Signale kann *man* als Marken anbringen.
Optical signals can be deposited in the form of marks.

2 Verb *lassen*

The combination of the verb *lassen* with *sich* and the infinitive of a verb is frequently used to express that something can be done. The English equivalent is *can be* and a past participle (cf. „*lassen*", p. 77).

Mehrere dieser Sinnesreize *lassen* sich kombinieren.
Several of these sensory stimuli can be *combined.*

3 Infinitive as a noun

The infinitive form of a verb can appear as a noun. It is then capitalized and is neuter in gender, i. e. it takes the article *das*. In English, a verbal noun ending in *-ing* usually corresponds to this form (cf. *Infinitive: Use*, p. 86).

Infinitive	Verbal Noun
empfangen *to receive*	das Empfangen *the receiving/ reception*
übertragen *to transmit*	das Übertragen *the transmitting/ transmission*
senden *to send, transmit*	das Senden *the sending/ transmitting/ transmission*

das *Empfangen, Übertragen* und *Senden* von Signalen
the reception *and* transmission *of signals*

9

Word formation

1 Suffix -er

The suffix -er designates a person doing a particular thing, a profession or an instrument (cf. *Suffixes in Nouns*, p. 141).

Goethe als Denk*er*
Goethe as a thinker

Bertrand Russell, Mathematik*er* und Schriftstell*er*
Bertrand Russell, mathematician and writer

vom Send*er* zum Empfäng*er*
from transmitter to receiver

2 Suffix -gemäß

The suffix -gemäß, added to nouns, forms adverbs or adjectives. It corresponds to *according to* (cf. *Suffixes in Adjectives*, p. 137).

definitions*gemäß*
by definition (according to definition)

3 Prepositions with *einander*

The pronoun *einander (one another)* can be connected to different prepositions, here to *nach (after)* and to *unter (under, among)*. The meaning of the preposition depends on the context:

Hängen sie (= die Sprachen) *untereinander* zusammen?
Are they related to one another?
Are they interrelated?

Wir besprechen nacheinander das Empfangen, Übertragen und Senden.
We shall discuss receiving and transmitting one after the other.
We shall discuss receiving and transmitting in turn.

Zur Verständigung *untereinander* benutzen Tiere...
In order to communicate with one another animals employ...

Text

Text: In an essay – originally a lecture held at the University of Freiburg in 1966 – with the title *Spiel und Sport (Games and Sport)* the author describes how games become sport by the addition of the notion of performance as a new category. He continues by suggesting that sport has arisen as a result of the Industrial Revolution. This passage is followed by the text below.

Quelle: Helmuth Plessner, Diesseits der Utopie, Copyright 1966 by Eugen Diederichs Verlag, Köln, S. 166 f.

Task 1:
Listen and follow the text. Then underline those German expressions in the text which correspond to the following English ones. Give the appropriate line number(s) as you do so.
The order of the passages in Englisch does not follow that of the German text.

Spiel und Sport

1 ... Traditionell für die alte vorindustrielle Welt war die ständische Gliederung. Das starre Gefüge existiert nicht mehr. Es wurde durch die politische Demokratisierung und durch die
5 Industrialisierung der Arbeitswelt in Richtung auf eine elitäre Gesellschaft umgeformt. Ihre Eliten sind Leistungseliten. Sie stellen das Produkt einer Auslese im freien Wettbewerb dar. Nicht die Herkunft soll mehr über die Aufstiegschancen entscheiden, sondern Begabung und Leistung sollen die
10 Besten an die Spitze bringen. Dieser Gedanke ist den Volksdemokratien totalitären Gepräges und den Demokratien der westlichen Welt gemeinsam. Und er erzeugt in beiden die gleichen Sehnsüchte und Unzufriedenheiten. Denn weder haben alle die gleichen Chancen – schon ihr Start ist verschie-
15 den – noch die gleichen Kräfte. Man will das verbessern. Aber die Macht der Geschichte und die menschlichen Schwächen werden dem elitären Prinzip immer wieder Schwierigkeiten machen. Tausende werden sagen: Warum nicht ich? Warum der Andere? Und sie suchen sich einen Ersatz.
20 Ihn bietet der Sport. Hier gibt es die große Chance, den Sprung nach vorn ins volle Rampenlicht der Öffentlichkeit, die exorbitante Karriere, das große Geschäft. ...

Line (s)

_____ *in the direction of an elitist society*

_____ *into the full glare* (lit.: *limelight*) *of publicity*

_____ *in free competition*

_____ *by the political democratization*

_____ *democracies of the Western World*

_____ *the power of history and human weaknesses*

_____ *the old preindustrial world*

_____ *the product of selection*

_____ *people's democracies with a totalitarian character*

Task 2:
Look for the five German sentences in the text and write each of them beside the English equivalent. The order of the items is the same as that in the text.

The rigid structure no longer exists.

_____

... talent and achievement should bring the best to the top.

_____

For neither do all individuals have the same opportunities (lit.:

chances) *... nor do they have the same strength.*

_____

Thousands will say: Why not me?

_____

Here is the big chance.

_____

Task 3:
Underline the five sentences in the text which you found in Task 2. Then read the text once again and try, on the basis of the underlined passages and other words which you already know, to reconstruct the probable train of thought of the author.

Task 4:
Here is the same text again divided into four short sections. Under each section there are some words from the text. Where no English equivalents are given you should supply them either from memory, by guesswork or deduction, or by looking them up in the *Basic Word List*. Then read the section through carefully and answer the questions on it. Discuss the solutions in class before you go on to do the next section in the same way.

> . . . Traditionell für die alte vorindustrielle Welt war die ständische Gliederung. Das starre Gefüge existierte nicht mehr. Es wurde durch die politische Demokratisierung und durch die
> 5 Industrialisierung der Arbeitswelt in Richtung auf eine elitäre Gesellschaft umgeformt. Ihre Eliten sind Leistungseliten.

die Gliederung, -en – _____
(noun, derived from the verb *gliedern*)

ihr- – its/her/their

die Leistung, -en – _____

ständisch – *corporate, corporative*

wurde . . . umgeformt – *was transformed*

a How was society organized before the Industrial Revolution?
b Are there still vestiges of this older order?
c What caused the transformation of society?
d What elites exist today?
e Whose elites are these? (Putting the question more formally: To what word does the expression *ihre* in front of *Eliten* refer?)

> Sie stellen das Produkt einer Auslese im freien Wettbewerb dar. Nicht die Herkunft soll mehr über die Aufstiegschancen entscheiden, sondern Begabung und Leistung sollen die
> 10 Besten an die Spitze bringen. Dieser Gedanke ist den Volksdemokratien totalitären Gepräges und den Demokratien der westlichen Welt gemeinsam.

der Aufstieg – *rise, advancement*

die Aufstiegschancen – *career prospects*

darstellen – _____

entscheiden über – _____

der Gedanke – _____

gemeinsam – _____

die Herkunft – _____

nicht mehr – *no longer*

sondern – _____

a How do these new elites arise?
b What role should social origin and achievement play today?
c On what point are People's Democracies and Western Democracies in agreement?

> Und er erzeugt in beiden die gleichen Sehnsüchte und Unzufriedenheiten. Denn weder haben alle die gleichen Chancen – schon ihr Start ist verschieden – noch die gleichen Kräfte. Man will das verbessern. Aber
> 15 die Macht der Geschichte und die menschlichen Schwächen werden dem elitären Prinzip immer wieder Schwierigkeiten machen.

aber – _____

beide – _____

erzeugen – _____

immer wieder – *again and again* (lit.: *ever again*)

(werden) machen – *(will)* _____

schon – here: *even*

die Schwierigkeit, -en – _____

die Sehnsucht – *longing, yearning*

die Unzufriedenheit – *dissatisfaction, discontent*

verbessern – _____

verschieden – _____

wollen (will) – _____

a What are the consequences of this idea in both East and West?
b Does equality of opportunity really exist?
c Whose start in life is different? (Putting the question more formally: To what word does the expression *ihr* in front of *Start* refer?)
d Why is it difficult to improve the situation?

> Tausende werden sagen: Warum nicht ich? Warum der Andere? Und sie suchen sich einen Ersatz.
> Ihn bietet der Sport. Hier gibt es die große Chance, den Sprung nach vorn ins volle Rampenlicht der Öffentlichkeit, 20 die exorbitante Karriere, das große Geschäft. . . .

andere   – _____

bieten   – _____

der Ersatz   – _____

das Geschäft – *business, deal*

ihn   – *him/ it*

nach vorn   – *forward, to the front*

der Sprung   – *jump, leap*

suchen   – _____

a How do many people react in this situation?
b What function does sport have today?
c What possibilities does sport offer?

Task 5:
Compare the following statements with the text and select one of the following alternatives:

a: The statement appears as such in the text or in other words. Indicate the relevant part of the text.

b: This statement does not appear in the text, and/or it contradicts the text. What does the text actually have to say on this point?

1 The society of the preindustrial era was rigidly stratified.
2 Elitist society brought about political democratization.
3 Performance-elites arise as a result of free competition.
4 If you have the "right" background, you have a greater chance of getting to the top.
5 The Eastern People's Democracies and the Western Democracies are based on the same fundamental principles.
6 In the Eastern People's Democracies people get to the top as a result of talent and performance rather than social origin; in the Western Democracies it is the other way round.
7 Emphasis on the performance-principle leads to dissatisfaction in both East and West.
8 It is wrong to maintain that all have equal opportunity and the same reserves of strength.
9 The elitist principle has overcome human weaknesses.
10 Sport has a "compensatory" function.
11 Many regard sport as an opportunity of quickly acquiring fame and riches.

Grammar

1 Auxiliary verb *werden*

The future form of the verb has two parts. It consists of the auxiliary verb *werden (to become)* and the infinitive of the verb (cf. *Future Tense*, p. 71).

Aber die Macht der Geschichte und die menschlichen Schwächen *werden* dem elitären Prinzip immer wieder Schwierigkeiten *machen*.
But the power of history and human weaknesses will *always* cause *difficulty for the elitist principle.*

Tausende *werden sagen:* . . .
Thousands will say: . . .

The auxiliary *werden* is also used to form the passive. In this case it combines with the past participle of the verb (cf. *Passive Voice*, p. 93).

Es (= das starre Gefüge) *wurde . . . umgeformt.*
It (= the rigid system) was transformed . . .

In chapter 15 there are further passive forms.

2 Word order (subject)

In addition to the normal word order subject – verb – object, the opposite order is also possible, i. e. object – verb – subject (cf. *Word Order (Subject)*, p. 109).

Optische Signale kann man als Marken anbringen.
One can fasten optical signals *in the form of marks.*

Sie suchen sich einen Ersatz. *Ihn bietet der Sport.*
They seek a substitute. Sport offers it.

These sentences are also unambiguous in German. The word *man* is always the subject; what is more *kann* is a singular form therefore the plural form *Signale* cannot be the subject. In the second example the clue is contained in the word *ihn*. It can only be the object. Moreover *Sport* is grammatically masculine, i. e. *der Sport* can only be the nominative form.

3 Possessive pronouns

The first person possessive pronouns are unambiguous: *Mein* corresponds to *my* (and *mine*), *unser* corresponds to *our* (and *ours*).

Alle meine Söhne.
All My Sons. (Arthur Miller)

Unsere kleine Stadt.
Our Little Town. (Thornton Wilder)

The third persons possessive pronouns are ambiguous in German. Their referents can only be determined by the context. *Sein* refers to a male person or to a masculine or neuter noun (articles *der* or *das*).

Einstein, sein Leben und sein Einfluß auf unsere Welt.
Einstein, his Life and his Influence upon our World.

Naturgeschichte des Lebens. Von seinen Anfängen bis zum Menschen.
Natural History of Life. From its Beginnings down to Man.

Ihr- refers to a female person, a feminine noun or a noun in the plural form (article *die*).

Jeanne Hersch gibt mit ihrem Buch eine Einführung...
In her book Jeanne Hersch provides an introduction...

Die Relativitätstheorie Einsteins und ihre physikalischen Grundlagen.
Einstein's Theory of Relativity and its Foundations in Physics.

Besteht eine innere Beziehung zwischen den Gegenständen und ihren Namen?
Is there an inner relationship between objects and their names?

Weder haben alle die gleichen Chancen – schon ihr Start ist verschieden...
Neither do all individuals have the same opportunities – even their start (in life) is different...

See also *Pronouns*, p. 31.

Word formation

1 Prefix *vor-*

Words with the prefix *vor-* cannot be usually understood on the basis of the basic meaning of their component parts (prefix and root). These should be regarded as independent words. This also applies to many words with other prefixes.

der Teil   but: der Vorteil   (and: der Nachteil)
   part   *advantage*   *disadvantage*

In some cases, however, the prefix *vor-* corresponds to the English *pre-* (cf. *Prefixes,* p. 133).

industriell – vorindustriell   geschichtlich – vorgeschichtlich
industrial   preindustrial   historic(al)   prehistoric

das Wort – das Vorwort
   word   *preface, foreword*

2 Suffix *-ung*

Nouns with the suffix *-ung* are feminine (c.f. *Suffixes in Nouns,* p. 144).

täuschen	die Täuschung
to deceive	*deception, illusion*
leisten	die Leistung
to achieve	*achievement*
einführen	die Einführung
to introduce	*introduction*
anordnen	die Anordnung
to arrange	*arrangement*
sich verständigen	die Verständigung
to communicate	*communication*
demokratisieren	die Demokratisierung
to democratize	*democratization*

Text

Text: In a short essay entitled *On the Inequality of Man* sociologist *Ralf Dahrendorf* criticizes romantic ideas and utopias. He shows why a society in which all of its members are absolutely equal is a sociological impossibility. – The text is from the final part of the essay.

Quelle: Ralf Dahrendorf, Pfade aus Utopia, R. Piper & Co Verlag, München 1967.

Über die Ungleichheit der Menschen

1 ... Natürlich ist Gleichheit vor dem Gesetz und gleiches Wahlrecht, sind gleiche Erziehungschancen und andere konkrete Gleichheiten möglich und auch wirklich. Aber der
5 Gedanke einer Gesellschaft, in der jeder Rangunterschied zwischen Menschen beseitigt ist, überschreitet das soziologisch Mögliche und hat seinen Ort allenfalls im Bereich dichterischer Phantasie. Wo immer politische Programme klassen- oder schichtenlose Gesellschaften, eine harmonische
10 Volksgemeinschaft gleichrangiger Genossen, die Reduktion aller Ungleichheiten auf funktionale Unterschiede oder ähnliches versprechen, haben wir auch darum Grund zum Mißtrauen, weil hinter nicht realisierbaren politischen Versprechungen gewöhnlich der Terror und die Unfreiheit lauern.
15 Wo immer aber herrschende Gruppen oder ihre Ideologen uns erzählen, in ihrer Gesellschaft seien tatsächlich alle gleich, können wir uns auf Orwells Vermutung verlassen, daß dort sicher „einige gleicher sind als andere".
...

Task 1:
Listen and follow the text, then answer the questions.

a Which adjective is typical of this text? – Underline the adjective and also all those words which are derived from it or enter into combination with it.
b An English writer is named in the text. Who is it? (Perhaps you may have read something by him.)

Task 2:
Find the German equivalents in the text and underline them. Give the appropriate line number(s) as you do so. Then discuss the solutions.

Line(s)

—— *equality before the law*

—— *other examples of equality*

—— *differences in status between human beings*

—— *that which is sociologically possible*

—— *poetic fantasy*

—— *societies without classes or strata*

—— *unrealizable promises by politicians*

—— Orwell's *suspicion that surely some are more equal than others*

Task 3:
Find the German equivalents in the passages quoted from the text and write them down.

> ...Natürlich ist Gleichheit vor dem Gesetz und gleiches Wahlrecht, sind gleiche Erziehungschancen und andere konkrete Gleichheiten möglich und auch wirklich.

other concrete equalities _____

equality before the law _____

equal educational opportunities _____

equal right to vote _____

possible _____

of course _____

real _____

also _____

> Aber der Gedanke einer Gesellschaft, in der jeder Rangunterschied zwischen Menschen beseitigt ist, überschreitet das soziologisch Mögliche und hat seinen Ort allenfalls im Bereich dichterischer Phantasie. [5]

between human beings _____

the thought of a society _____

every difference in status _____

in the sphere of poetic fantasy _____

the sociologically possible _____

transcends _____

eliminated _____

at the most _____

place _____

Task 4:
Read through the preceding two sentences from the text once again and answer the questions.

a Which forms of equality are attainable within a given society (according to the text)?
b On what point do the opinions of sociologists and writers differ?

55

Task 5:
Find the German equivalents in the passage from the text quoted below and underline them.

class- or strataless societies
the reduction of all inequalities to functional differences
grounds for mistrust
behind unrealizable promises
terror and lack of freedom
dominant groups or their ideologists
we can rely on Orwell's *suspicion*
some are more equal than others

. . . Wo immer politische Programme klassen- und schichtenlose
    Wherever

Gesellschaften, eine harmonische Volksgemeinschaft gleichran-

giger Genossen, die Reduktion aller Ungleichheiten auf funktio-

nale Unterschiede oder ähnliches versprechen, haben wir auch
    or their like   promise

darum   Grund zum Mißtrauen, weil   hinter nicht reali-
(therefore)   *because*

sierbaren politischen Versprechungen gewöhnlich der Terror
          generally

und die Unfreiheit lauern. Wo immer aber herrschende Grup-
      lurk

pen oder ihre Ideologen uns erzählen, in ihrer Gesellschaft sei-
        us tell   their   are

en tatsächlich alle gleich, können wir uns auf Orwells Vermutung
  in fact

verlassen, daß dort sicher   „einige gleicher sind als an-
        that there we can be sure

dere".

Task 6:
Look for the contextually appropriate English meaning of the words given below in the *Basic Word List.* Then state as precisely as possible the meaning of the expression quoted (lines 9–10 of the text).

. . . eine harmonische Volksgemeinschaft gleichrangiger Genossen . . .

das Volk ———————— die Gemeinschaft ————————

der Rang ———————— der Genosse   *comrade; com-*
                                panion

Task 7:
Read the passage quoted from the text (in Task 5) once again and answer the questions.

a What do many political programmes promise?
b Why is it advisable to exercise caution with regard to such promises?
c How should we react to an ideology which claims to have established a society of equals?

Task 8:
Underline all those nouns which, on the basis of their meaning or grammatical endings, are clearly plural forms in the text.

> . . . Natürlich ist Gleichheit vor dem Gesetz und gleiches Wahlrecht, sind gleiche Erziehungschancen und andere konkrete Gleichheiten möglich und auch wirklich. Aber der Gedanke einer Gesellschaft, in der jeder Rangunterschied [5] zwischen Menschen beseitigt ist, überschreitet das soziologisch Mögliche und hat seinen Ort allenfalls im Bereich dichterischer Phantasie. Wo immer politische Programme klassen- oder schichtenlose Gesellschaften, eine harmonische Volksgemeinschaft gleichrangiger Genossen, die Reduktion aller [10] Ungleichheiten auf funktionale Unterschiede oder ähnliches versprechen, haben wir auch darum Grund zum Mißtrauen, weil hinter nicht realisierbaren politischen Versprechungen gewöhnlich der Terror und die Unfreiheit lauern. Wo immer aber herrschende Gruppen oder ihre Ideologen uns erzählen, [15] in ihrer Gesellschaft seien tatsächlich alle gleich, können wir uns auf Orwells Vermutung verlassen, daß dort sicher „einige gleicher sind als andere".

Task 9:
Compare the following statements with the text and select one of the following alternatives:

a This statement appears as such in the text or in other words. Indicate where it can be found in the text.

b This statement does not appear in the text, and/or it contradicts the text. What does the text actually have to say on this point?

1 Equality before the law is something natural.
2 Equal educational opportunities are a possibility but seldom realized in actual practice.
3 A society without social strata is undesirable.
4 A society with no differences in status between its members is a sociological impossibility.
5 Through their powers of imagination writers promote social progress.
6 Politicians advocating a classless society should be regarded with suspicion.
7 Unrealizable political promises necessarily lead to inequality.
8 Those in power wish all in their society to be equal.
9 Ideologists who have in fact created a society of equals have shown *Orwell's* hypothesis to be false.

Grammar

1 Anticipatory *darum/deshalb* **with** *weil*

Unlike English subordinate clauses, subordinate clauses in German introduced by *weil (because, since)* are sometimes preceded by *darum* or *deshalb (therefore, because of that)* which point to the following clause of reason (cf. *"weil"*, p. 108).

. . . haben wir auch *darum* Grund zum Mißtrauen, *weil* hinter nicht realisierbaren politischen Versprechungen gewöhnlich der Terror und die Unfreiheit *lauern.*
. . . *we have grounds for mistrust*, since *terror and lack of freedom generally* lurk *behind unrealisable political promises.*

2 Conjunction *wo immer*

Clauses introduced by *wo immer (wherever)* are subordinate clauses, and the finite verb form takes end position:

Wo immer politische Programme klassen- oder schichtenlose Gesellschaften . . . oder ähnliches *versprechen,* . . .
Wherever *political programmes* promise *class- or strataless societies . . . or their like,* . . .

Wo immer aber herrschende Gruppen oder ihre Ideologen uns *erzählen* . . .
But wherever *dominant groups or their ideologists* tell *us* . . .

3 Reflexive pronoun *uns*

The verb *verlassen* means *to leave, to abandon.* The text, however, contains the reflexive verb *sich verlassen (auf)* and this means *to rely (on).* The reflexive pronoun *sich* only occurs in the third person. In the first person the reflexive and personal pronouns are identical *(mich – me/myself, uns – us/ourselves)*:

. . . können wir *uns auf* Orwells Vermutung *verlassen* . . .
. . . *we can* rely on *Orwell's suspicion* . . .

4 Prepositions

Some common prepositions coalesce with the definite article:
beim = bei dem; im = in dem; ins = in das; vom = von dem; zum = zu dem; zur = zu der

Sie kommmen gleichzeitig *beim* Empfänger an.
They arrive at the *receiver at the same time.*

im Bereich dichterischer Phantasie
in the *sphere of poetic fantasy*

der Sprung *ins* volle Rampenlicht der Öffentlichkeit
the leap into the *full glare of publicity*

vom Sender *zum* Empfänger
from *transmitter* to *receiver*

zur Verständigung untereinander
in order to *communicate with one another*

Word formation

1 Suffixes *-isch, -ig, -lich*

The number of non-derivative adjectives is relatively small (cf. *Suffixes in Adjectives*, p. 135). Examples from the texts:

gleich   sicher   frei kurz groß
equal; same certain, sure free short great, big, tall

Most adjectives are formed with the aid of suffixes. The most frequent of these are *-isch, -ig, -lich* (cf. *Suffixes in Adjectives*, pp. 137–138). Examples from the texts:

soziologisch politisch dichterisch (from: Dichter) möglich
sociological political poetic   poet   possible

gleichrangig   gleichzeitig   wirklich ähnlich gewöhnlich
equal in rank, simultaneous,   real   similar usual,
of equal status at the same time   ordinary

2 Suffix *-los*

The suffix *-los* corresponds to the English suffix *-less* (cf. *Suffixes in Adjectives*, p. 138). Examples from the texts:

sinnlos (der Sinn) schichtenlos (die Schicht)
senseless   sense   strataless   stratum

klassenlos (die Klasse)
classless   class

3 Suffix *-schaft*

Nouns formed with the suffix *-schaft* are feminine (cf. *Suffixes in Nouns*, p. 143). Examples from the texts:

die Gemeinschaft (gemein)
  community   common

die Gesellschaft   (der Geselle)
  society; company   companion

die *Wissenschaft (das Wissen)*
  science   knowledge

die Wirtschaft (der Wirt)
  economy   landlord; host

4 Suffixes *-heit, -keit*

Nouns formed with the suffixes *-heit* or *-keit* are feminine (cf. *Suffixes in Nouns*, pp. 142–143). Examples from the textes:

die Freiheit (frei)   die Gleichheit (gleich)
  freedom free   equality   equal

die Zufriedenheit (zufrieden)
  contentedness, content,
  satisfaction   satisfied

die Schwierigkeit (schwierig)   die Persönlichkeit (persönlich)
  difficulty   difficult   personality   personal

5 Prefix *un-*

The negative prefix *un- (un-, in-)* appears in adjectives, adverbs and nouns (cf. *Prefixes,* p. 131). Examples from the texts:

möglich unmöglich
possible impossible

Freiheit Unfreiheit
freedom lack of freedom

Gleichheit Ungleichheit
equality inequality

Zufriedenheit Unzufriedenheit
satisfaction discontent, dissatisfaction

Text

Geographische Mobilität

Das Bevölkerungsbild Europas ist nicht nur das Ergebnis einer langen natürlichen Bevölkerungsentwicklung, sondern auch in gleicher Weise die Folge großer *Wanderungsbewegungen,* die bis in die Gegenwart nicht abgerissen sind. Es gab Zeiten, in denen sich ganze Völker und Volksgruppen gleichzeitig in Bewegung setzten, was für die Abwanderungs- und Aufnahmegebiete schwere politische, ökonomische und sozial-psychologische Konsequenzen hatte. Sogenannte „natürliche" *Ursachen und Anlässe* wie Klimawandel, Bedrohung durch das Meer und Erschöpfung der Ressourcen waren nicht die einzigen; dazu kamen noch Übervölkerung, Wandel des Lebensstils sowie politische, religiöse und ökonomische Zwänge. . . .

die Wanderung, -en – migration

Wanderungsbewegungen – _____

Ursachen und Anlässe _____

Text: In a handbook on Europe the chapter on the population and peoples of Europe begins with the natural development of the population. It then goes on to deal with the other factors which have contributed to the present day picture of the population of Europe.
This text is the beginning of this second section, which is concerned with the effects of geographical mobility.

Quelle: W. Sperling/A. Karger (Hrsg.), Fischer Länderkunde: Europa, Fischer Taschenbuch, Bd. 6127, Frankfurt 1978, S. 68.

Task 1:
Listen and follow the text. With the help of the *Basic Word List* find out the meaning of the three nouns which are printed in italics.

Task 2:
Find examples in the text of compounds consisting of two nouns (such as *Wanderungsbewegungen*) and write them down with their English equivalents.

1 _____	– _____
2 _____	– _____
3 _____	– _____
4 Abwanderungs_____	– *emigration* _____
5 Aufnahme_____	– *immigration* _____
6 _____	– _____
7 _____	– _____

Task 3:
Find the seven finite verb forms in the text and put a circle round each of them. – To which grammatical tense do you think the last five forms might belong? What are their probable English equivalents? (These five verbs are cognates.)

Task 4:
Listen and follow the text once again. Then find the German equivalents in the text and underline them. Discuss the solutions.

a *overpopulation, change in lifestyle as well as political pressures*
b *the consequence of great migratory movements*
c *the result of a long development*
d *threats from the sea and the exhausting of resources*

Task 5:
Find the German equivalents in the text and write them down; then discuss the solutions.

a *periods in which whole peoples began to move* (lit. *set themselves in motion) at the same time*

_____

b *for the regions which were abandoned* (lit. *for the emigration-regions)*

_____

c *movements which have not ceased until the present day*

_____

Task 6:
Read the text once again with the aid of the words given.

1 ## Geographische Mobilität

Das Bevölkerungsbild Europas ist nicht nur das Ergebnis einer langen natürlichen Bevölkerungsentwicklung, sondern auch in gleicher Weise die Folge großer *Wanderungsbewegungen,* die bis in die Gegenwart nicht abgerissen sind. Es gab
5 Zeiten, in denen sich ganze Völker und Volksgruppen gleichzeitig in Bewegung setzten, was für die Abwanderungs- und Aufnahmegebiete schwere politische, ökonomische und sozial-psychologische Konsequenzen hatte. Sogenannte
10 „natürliche" *Ursachen und Anlässe* wie Klimawandel, Bedrohung durch das Meer und Erschöpfung der Ressourcen waren nicht die einzigen; dazu kamen noch Übervölkerung, Wandel des Lebensstils sowie politische, religiöse und ökonomische Zwänge. . . .

Line		
2	nur	– *only*
4	auch	– *also*
4	Weise	– *way, manner*
5	Es gab . . .	– *There were . . .*
7	was	– *which*
8	schwer	– *grave, serious*
10	wie	– *like*
12	die einzigen	– *the only ones*
12	dazu	– *to these*
12	noch	– *in addition*

Task 7:
Use information supplied in the text to fill in the blanks.

1. The present distribution of peoples in Europe is the result of

    a _____

    b _____

2. In former periods whole peoples and ethnic groups

    _____

3. These migrations had serious consequences for

    a _____

    b _____

4. "Natural" causes for the migrations were

    a _____

    b _____

    c _____

5. Further causes were

    a _____

    b _____

    c _____

1 ## Frühgriechische Literatur

Wir nehmen es als selbstverständlich, daß es in den abendländischen Literaturen verschiedene Dichtungsarten nebeneinander gibt, das Epos, die Lyrik und das Drama. Bei den
5 Griechen, die diese Dichtgattungen als Formen großer Poesie geschaffen haben und durch deren direkten oder indirekten Einfluß sie sich bei den europäischen Völkern entfaltet haben, blühten sie nicht neben-, sondern nacheinander: Als das Epos verklang, hob die Lyrik an, und als die Lyrik ihrem
10 Ende entgegenging, entstand das Drama. Im Lande ihres Ursprungs waren also diese Dichtungsarten Leistung und Ausdruck einer bestimmten geschichtlichen Situation . . .

Text:
This text is from a book by the classical philologist *Bruno Snell* about the Greek origins of European thinking. It is the beginning of the chapter *The Awaking of the Personality in Early Greek Lyric Poetry.*

Quelle: Bruno Snell, Die Entdeckung des Geistes, Vandenhoeck & Ruprecht, Göttingen 1975, S. 56.

Task 1:
Listen and follow the text; then give the English equivalents of the two following compounds (using the *Basic Word List*).

Dichtung – *poetry, literature*;

Dichtungsarten – _____ ;

Dichtgattungen – _____

Task 2:
Read the text once again and put a circle round all literary terms. Discuss the solutions.

Task 3:
Find the German equivalents in the text and write them down.

a *with the Greeks*

_____

b *in Western Literatures*

_____

c *in the land of their origin*

_____

d *with (= among) the European peoples*

_____

e *expression of a particular historical situation*

_____

f *as forms of great poetry*

_____

g *not side by side* (lit. *beside one another*), *but after one another*

_____

h *through whose direct or indirect influence*

_____

Task 4:
Read the text once again and try, on the basis of the passages in task 3 and other words which you already know, to reconstruct the probable train of thought of the author.

Task 5:
Find the German equivalents in the text and underline them.

a *when the . . . approached its end, the . . . arose*
b *that there are various literary genres*
c *they developed* (lit. *have unfolded themselves*)
d *we regard it as being natural* (lit. *take it as natural*)
e *when the . . . fell silent* (lit. *faded*), *the . . . raised its voice* (lit. *commenced*)
f *who created* (lit. *have created*) *these literary genres*
g *these literary genres were the achievement and expression*
h *they flourished not together, but after one another*

Wir nehmen es als selbstverständlich, daß es in den abendländischen Literaturen verschiedene Dichtungsarten nebeneinander gibt, das Epos, die Lyrik und das Drama. Bei den Griechen, die diese Dichtgattungen als Formen großer Poesie geschaffen haben und durch deren indirekten oder direkten Einfluß sie sich bei den europäischen Völkern entfaltet haben, blühten sie nicht neben-, sondern nacheinander: Als das Epos verklang, hob die Lyrik an, und als die Lyrik ihrem Ende entgegenging, entstand das Drama. Im Lande ihres Ursprungs waren also diese Dichtungsarten Leistung und Ausdruck einer bestimmten geschichtlichen Situation. . . .

Task 6:
Answer the questions relying exclusively on information supplied in the text.

a What appears self-evident to us in our literature?
b What is the connection between the European and Greek Literatures?
c What can be said about the combination of the three literary genres in Ancient Greece?
d What does *also* (a "false friend") mean in the last sentence of the text?

61

Grammar

1 Past tense

The past can be indicated by a particular ending or by a change in the vowel in the verb stem.
Regular verbs have in the first and third person singular the ending -te and in the first and third person plural the ending -ten.
Irregular verbs show vowel changes and have in the first and third person singular no ending and in the first and third person plural the ending -en (cf. *Verbs: Past Tense,* p. 66).

– blühen *(flourish)*
Bei den Griechen blühten sie nicht neben-, sondern nacheinander.
With the Greeks they flourished not together, but after one another.

– verklingen *(fall silent),* anheben *(commence)*
Als das Epos verklang, hob die Lyrik an.
When the epic fell silent, the lyric poem raised its voice.

– entgegengehen *(approach),* entstehen *(arise)*
Als die Lyrik ihrem Ende entgegenging, entstand das Drama.
As the lyric poem approached its end, the drama arose.

– es gibt *(there is/there are)*
Es gab Zeiten, in denen sich ganze Völker . . . in Bewegung setzten.
There were periods when whole peoples began to move . . .

– haben *(have)*
. . ., was schwere politische, ökonomische und sozial-psychologische Konsequenzen hatte.
. . . which had serious political, economic and socio-psychological consequences.

– sind *(are),* kommen *(come)*
Sogenannte „natürliche" Ursachen und Anlässe waren nicht die einzigen; dazu kamen noch Übervölkerung, Wandel des Lebensstils . . .
So-called "natural" causes and reasons were not the only ones; to these were added (lit. *came in addition) overpopulation, changes in lifestyle . . .*

2 Various uses of *als*

The word *als* appears as the equivalent of *as, than* or *when.*

a   Goethe als Denker.
Goethe as a thinker.

Optische Signale kann man als Marken anbringen.
Optical signals can be fastened in the form of marks.

Bei den Griechen, die diese Dichtgattungen als Formen großer Poesie geschaffen haben, . . .
With the Greeks who created these literary genres as forms of great poetry . . .

Wir nehmen es als selbstverständlich, daß . . .
We regard it as being natural that . . .

b   Wir können uns auf Orwells Vermutung verlassen, daß dort „einige gleicher sind als andere".
We can rely on Orwell's suspicion that there "some are more equal than others".

. . . erscheint der innere Kreis viel größer, wenn er im Mittelpunkt kleiner Kreise steht, als wenn größere ihn umgeben.
. . . the inner circle appears much bigger if it is at the centre of small circles than if bigger ones surround it.

c   Als das Epos verklang, hob die Lyrik an.
When the epic fell silent, the lyric poem raised its voice.

Und als die Lyrik ihrem Ende entgegenging, entstand das Drama.
And when the lyric poem approached its end, the drama arose.

3 Relative pronouns

Most of the relative pronoun forms are the same as the definite articles (cf. *Relative Pronouns,* pp. 32–33). Relative pronouns introduce dependent clauses.

. . . der scheinbar kleinere Kreis, *der* von fünf großen Kreisen eingeschlossen ist.
. . . the apparently smaller circle, which *is surrounded by five large circles.*

Signale und Nachrichten, *die* vom Sender zum Empfänger gehen, . . .
Signals and information which *are conveyed from transmitter to receiver . . .*

Alle Arten von Signalen, für *deren* Empfang sie Sinnesorgane haben, . . .
Signals of all kinds for the reception of which *they are equipped with sensory organs . . .*

Eine Gesellschaft, in *der* jeder Rangunterschied zwischen Menschen beseitigt ist, . . .
A society in which *every difference in status between human beings has been eliminated . . .*

Es gab Zeiten, in *denen* sich ganze Völker . . . in Bewegung setzten, . . .
There were periods in which *whole peoples . . . began to move . . .*

Bei den Griechen, *die* diese Dichtgattungen als Formen großer Poesie geschaffen haben und durch *deren* direkten oder indirekten Einfluß sie sich . . . entfaltet haben, . . .
With the Greeks who *created these literary genres as forms of great poetry and as a result* of whose *direct or indirect influence they developed . . .*

Word formation

1 Compound words

Compound nouns are, for the most part, constructed according to the pattern noun + noun. Sometimes two nouns are simply written as one (cf. *Compound Words*, pp. 120–123).

Klima	Wandel	Klimawandel
climate	*change*	*change of climate*

Wahl	Recht	Wahlrecht
election	*right*	*right to vote*

Frequently letters are added between the two nouns, above all *-s-/-es-*, or else *-n-/-en-*.

Leben	Stil	Lebensstil
life	*style*	*lifestyle*

Sinn	Organ	Sinnesorgan
sense	*organ*	*sensory organ*

Leistung	Elite	Leistungselite
achievement	*elite*	*elite of achievement*

Rampe	Licht	Rampenlicht
ramp/forestage	*light*	*footlights/limelight*

In some cases the last letter of the first noun is dropped, mostly the letter *-e*.

Schule	Wesen	Schulwesen
school	*being/essence*	*school system*

In some compounds the first noun appears in the plural.

Nachricht	Kanal	Nachrichtenkanal
piece of news	*channel*	*information channel*

Compound nouns of the type adjective + noun occur less frequently.

sozial	Arbeiter	Sozialarbeiter
social	*worker*	*social worker*

gesamt	Gebiet	Gesamtgebiet
whole/entire	*area/field*	*whole field*

2 Basic word *Volk*

das Volk, plural: die Völker (*people, peoples*)

Compounds:

Volksgruppe (*ethnic group*); Volksgemeinschaft (*national community*); Volksdemokratie (*people's democracy*)

Derivatives:

Bevölkerung (*population*); Übervölkerung (*overpopulation*)

13

Text

Text: This text is the beginning of a chapter on the development and aims of family therapy and is from a book by the psychoanalyst *Richter* on the origins, structure and treatment of conflicts within marriage and the family.

Quelle: Horst-Eberhard Richter, Patient Familie, Copyright © 1979 by Rowohlt Verlag GmbH, Reinbek bei Hamburg.

Task 1:
Answer the questions according to your knowledge.
a What do you understand by the expression *Familientherapie*?
b Which other form of therapy is known to you?
c Which of these forms is the older one?

Task 2:
Listen and follow the text; then put a circle round all words having to do with *Familie* and *Therapie*.

Task 3:
Each of the following statements represents a summary of a sentence from the text. Arrange these statements in the order in which they appear in the text and give the numbers of the relevant line(s) of the text in each case.

Task 4:
Find the German equivalents in the text and write them down.

a *for a long time*

b *several members of a family*

c *either alone or with the aid of the doctor*

d *the actual patient*

e *that each was allocated his own therapist* (lit. "*each received for himself his own therapist*")

f *the model of the exclusive dual relationship*

Task 5:
Find the verbs in the text and underline them. (They are given here in the infinitive.)

achten (auf)	sich bemühen (um)	sich ergeben	sich halten (an)	sollen
bekommen	sich beschäftigen (mit)	erhalten	sein	wünschen

Familientherapie 1

Wie jede andere Heilkunde beschäftigte sich auch die Psychotherapie über lange Zeit nur mit dem einzelnen kranken Menschen. Wenn sich ergab, daß in ein psychisches Problem zugleich mehrere Angehörige einer Familie verstrickt waren, 5
so bemühte sich die Familie entweder allein oder mit Hilfe des Arztes zunächst um eine Klärung der Frage, wer denn nun der *eigentliche Patient* sein und eine Behandlung bekommen solle. Ergab sich, daß zugleich mehrere an dem Konflikt beteiligte Familienmitglieder für sich eine Therapie wünsch- 10
ten, so achtete man in der Regel darauf, daß jeder für sich seinen eigenen Therapeuten erhielt. Denn alle Varianten unserer traditionellen Medizin halten sich streng an das Modell der exklusiven Zweierbeziehung Arzt−Patient.

Heilkunde	− *medicine* (lit. *science of healing*)
Arzt	− *doctor*
Behandlung	− *treatment*

Line(s)

____ Traditional medicine adheres to the doctor-patient dual relationship.

____ Psychotherapy was only concerned with the individual patient.

____ If several members of a family desired individual therapy at the same time, each was allocated his own therapist.

____ If several members of a family were involved in a psychological problem, they tried to determine who was the actual patient.)

64

Task 6:
Look up the verbs in the *Basic Word List* and enter a suitable English equivalent in the gaps provided. Watch out for verbs in the past tense.

a . . . *beschäftigte sich* die Psychotherapie *mit* dem einzelnen . . .

. . . *psychotherapy* _____ _____
the individual . . .

b Wenn *sich ergab,* . . .

If it _____ , . . .

c daß mehrere . . . verstrickt *waren,* . . .

that several . . . _____ *embroiled* . . .

d so *bemühte sich* die Familie . . .

then the family _____ . . .

e wer der eigentliche Patient *sein* und eine Behandlung *bekommen solle.*

who _____ _____ *the actual patient and*

_____ *(a) treatment.*

f *Ergab sich,* daß mehrere . . . eine Therapie *wünschten* . . .

If it _____ *that several* . . .

_____ *a therapy* . . .

g . . . daß jeder . . . seinen eigenen Therapeuten *erhielt.*

. . . *that each* . . . _____ *his own*
therapist.

h Denn alle Varianten . . . *halten sich an* das Modell . . .

For all variants _____ *the model* . . .

Wie jede andere Heilkunde beschäftigte sich auch die Psychotherapie über lange Zeit nur mit dem einzelnen kranken Menschen. Wenn sich ergab, daß in ein psychisches Problem
5 zugleich mehrere Angehörige einer Familie verstrickt waren, so bemühte sich die Familie entweder allein oder mit Hilfe des Arztes zunächst um eine Klärung der Frage, wer denn nun der *eigentliche Patient* sein und eine Behandlung bekommen solle. Ergab sich, daß zugleich mehrere an dem Konflikt
10 beteiligte Familienmitglieder für sich eine Therapie wünschten, so achtete man in der Regel darauf, daß jeder für sich seinen eigenen Therapeuten erhielt. Denn alle Varianten unserer traditionellen Medizin halten sich streng an das Modell der exklusiven Zweierbeziehung Arzt−Patient.

achten (darauf)	– *to pay attention (to the fact)*
beteiligt (an)	– *involved (in)*
Frage	– *question*
Klärung	– *clarification*
krank	– *ill, sick*
Mitglied, -er	– *member*
in der Regel	– *as a rule*
streng	– *strict(ly), severe(ly)*
wie	– *how; like; as*
zugleich	– *at the same time*
zunächst	– *first (of all)*

Task 7:
Read the text once again and answer the questions.

a To which discipline is psychotherapy allocated at the beginning of the text?
b What did psychotherapy long have in common with other branches of medicine?
c What could complicate a psychological problem?
d What did the family do in such a case?
e What was supposed to happen to the actual patient?
f In which case were several therapists necessary?
g Which rule is adhered to by traditional medicine?
h How will this chapter go on after this introduction?

Task 8:
Summarize the text in your own words.

Grammar

1 Reflexive pronoun *sich*

The reflexive pronoun *sich* appears with the so-called reflexive verbs (cf. *Reflexive Verbs*, p. 92).

Das Buch gründet sich auf eingehende Studien . . .
The book is based (lit. *founds itself*) *on thorough studies* . . .

Alle Varianten . . . halten sich streng an das Modell . . .
All variants adhere (lit. *keep themselves*) *strictly to the model* . . .

The reflexive pronoun *sich* corresponds to the English *himself/ herself/itself/themselves* (cf. *Personal Pronouns*, pp. 34–35).

. . . daß mehrere Familienmitglieder für sich eine Therapie wünschten.
. . . *that several of the family members desired individual therapy* (lit. *desired a therapy for themselves*).

2 Prepositions

Prepositions occur in expressions indicating place, time, manner, or cause:

in einigen Ländern;   *im* Mittelalter;   *mit* Hilfe des Arztes;
in *some countries*   in *the Middle Ages*   with *the aid of the doctor*

infolge der Anordnung der Pfeile
as a result *of the arrangement of the arrows*

Prepositions also occur together with a verb, a noun, or an adjective:

Grund zum Mißtrauen
grounds for *mistrust*

in ein psychisches Problem *verstrickt*
embroiled in *a psychological problem*

Jede Form sozialen Lebens *basiert auf* Verständigung.
Each form of social life is based on *communication*.

. . . *beschäftigte sich* die Psychotherapie *mit* dem einzelnen kranken Menschen.
. . . *psychotherapy* was concerned with *the individual patient*.

3 Adverb *darauf*

Da- or *dar-* combined with a preposition sometimes precedes *daß* (cf. Da-*compounds*, p. 41).

. . . achtete man in der Regel *darauf, daß* jeder für sich seinen eigenen Therapeuten erhielt.
. . . *it was generally arranged* that *each was allocated his own therapist.*
(darauf achten, daß – *to take care that*)

4 Conditional clauses with/without *wenn*

Conditional clauses introduced by *wenn* (*if*) are sometimes followed by *so (then)* at the beginning of the main clause (cf. *List of Common Conjunctions*, pp. 108–109).

Wenn sich ergab, daß in ein psychisches Problem zugleich mehrere Angehörige einer Familie verstrickt waren, *so* bemühte sich die Familie . . .
If *it turned out that several members of a family were together involved in a psychological problem*, then *the family tried* . . .

There are also conditional clauses without *wenn*. They begin with the finite verb. The following main clause often begins with *so (then)* (cf. *Conditional Clauses without "wenn"*, p. 102).

Ergab sich, daß mehrere an dem Konflikt beteiligte Familienmitglieder für sich eine Therapie wünschten, *so* achtete man in der Regel darauf, daß . . .
If *it* turned out *that several of the family members involved in the conflict desired individual therapy*, then *it was generally arranged that* . . .

5 Indirect questions

Indirect (or dependent) questions are subordinate clauses, i.e. the verb occupies end position.
Compare direct and indirect questions:

Warum *ist* die Neue Musik so schwer zu verstehen?
Why is *Modern Music so difficult to understand?*

. . . die Frage, wer der eigentliche Patient sein und eine Behandlung bekommen *solle*.*
. . . *the question who* should *be the actual patient and receive treatment.*

---

* *solle*, a subjunctive form, appears here (instead of *soll*) to emphasize that the author is quoting a question asked by someone else, in this case the family concerned (cf. *Reported Speech*, p. 97).

Word formation

1 Basic word *zwei*

zwei klassische Beispiele optischer Täuschung
two classical examples of optical illusion

das Modell der exklusiven Zweierbeziehung
the model of the exclusive dual relationship

im zweiten Beispiel
in the second example

(cf. *Suffixes in Adjectives, -t,* p. 140)

2 Words which are easily confused

a *eigene, einige, einzelne, einzige*
. . . daß „*einige* gleicher sind als andere".
. . . *that* "some *are more equal than others".*

. . . daß jeder seinen *eigenen* Therapeuten erhielt.
. . . *that each was allocated his* own *therapist.*

. . . mit dem *einzelnen* kranken Menschen.
. . . *with the* individual *patient.*

Sogenannte „natürliche" Ursachen waren nicht die *einzigen.*
So-called "natural" causes were not the only ones.

b *mehr, mehrere*
immer *mehr* Schüler, Eltern und Lehrer
more *and* more (lit. *always more) schoolchildren, parents, and teachers*

Das starre Gefüge existiert *nicht mehr.*
The rigid system no longer *exists.*

mehrere Angehörige einer Familie
several *members of a family*

Text

Text: Short description of a book

Quelle: Publisher's catalogue

1 **Alexander von Humboldt,
Abenteuer eines Weltreisenden**
Von Humboldt legte die Grundlage der modernen Geographie und gilt als Begründer der Klimalehre, der Lehre vom
5 Erdmagnetismus, der Meereskunde und der Geologie. – Originaltexte herausgegeben und mit Kommentaren versehen
von Hedwig Wanasek. 336 Seiten mit zeitgenössischen Illustrationen.

Abenteuer, -	– adventure
Reisender	– traveller
legen	– to lay
gelten	– to be considered
Begründer	– founder
Lehre	– theory, science
Meer	– sea, ocean
Meereskunde	– oceanography
herausgegeben	– edited
versehen	– supplied
zeitgenössisch	– contemporary

Task:
Listen and follow the text, then answer the questions.
a   What information about *Alexander von Humboldt* is supplied
   in the text?
b   What do we learn about the book?
c   What is *Hedwig Wanasek*'s contribution to the book?

Text: This text is from an essay by the geographer *Albrecht Haushofer* (1903–1945). It appeared in 1935 in a monthly magazine and praises the achievements of the *Humboldt* brothers. While *Wilhelm von Humboldt* (1767–1835) was an important scholar of the humanities and is known as the reformer of the German educational system, his brother *Alexander von Humboldt* (1769–1859) distinguished himself in the field of the natural sciences.

Quelle: Albrecht Haushofer, Die Brüder Humboldt. In: Deutsche Rundschau, hrsgg. von Rudolf Pechel, Rütten & Loening Verlag, Hamburg 1961, S. 384–385.

1 **Alexander von Humboldt**

. . .

Die „zweite Entdeckung Amerikas" war etwas Einzigartiges,
weil Alexander anders war als die Menschen seiner Zeit. Er
5 ist der erste Forschungsreisende großen Stils, dem zugleich
die Gabe leidenschaftlicher Nüchternheit der Tatsachenforschung und die Fähigkeit zusammenschauender und wagemutiger Phantasie gegeben waren. So ist er der Vater einer
modernen Naturbetrachtung und Naturbeschreibung geworden. Eine Reihe von Einzelwissenschaften, als wichtigste
10 vielleicht die Pflanzengeographie, nimmt von ihm ihren Ausgang. In den von ihm bereisten Ländern des spanischen
Amerika lebt sein Name als der eines Begründers ihrer
Kenntnis von sich selbst. Nach einem fünfjährigen Aufenthalt
in den Ländern, die heute Venezuela, Kolumbien, Ekuador,
15 Mexiko und Kuba heißen, mit einer Fülle von Ergebnissen
aus dem Bereich von Botanik und Zoologie, Klimatologie,
Geophysik und Länderkunde verläßt er mit seinem treuen
Begleiter Bonpland Ende April 1805 die Insel Kuba, um über
20 Nordamerika nach Europa zurückzukehren.

. . .

Task 1:
Listen and follow the text; then answer the questions.

a   What are the names of the countries in which Alexander von
   Humboldt travelled?
b   What expression is used generally in the text for all of these
   countries?
c   How many years did he stay in these countries?
d   When did he leave these regions?
e   Which were the last two places to be visited by him before
   his return to Europe? (*Insel* means . . .?)
f   Which six individual sciences are mentioned in the text?
g   What might the last of these to be mentioned mean? (Think
   of the compounds *Heilkunde, Meereskunde*.)
h   America was first "discovered" in 1492. What does the
   zweite Entdeckung Amerikas (line 3) mean?
i   What does the author probably wish to convey by means of
   this expression?

Task 2:
Find the German equivalents in the text and underline them.

a   *He is the first explorer* (lit. *research traveller*) *in the grand style*
b   *In the countries of Spanish America, in which he travelled,* . . .
c   . . . *as that of a founder of their knowledge of themselves*
d   . . . *in the countries which are today called* . . .
e   . . . *he leaves with his faithful companion Bonpland* . . .

Task 3:
Find the German equivalents in the text and write them down.

a *. . . because Alexander was different from the people of his time.*

b *Thus he has become the father of modern description of nature.*

c *A number (lit. row) of individual sciences . . .*

d *After a five-year sojourn . . .*

e *. . . with a whole host (lit. a fullness/a wealth) of results from the sphere of botany . . .*

f *. . . in order to return to Europe via North America.*

Task 4:
Complete the vocabulary list on the text by consulting the *Basic Word List.*

etwas	– _____
einzigartig	– *unique*
Forschung	– *research*
dem . . . gegeben waren	– *who was endowed with . . . (lit. to whom . . . were given)*
zugleich	– _____
Gabe	– *gift*
leidenschaftlich	– *passionate*
Nüchternheit	– *sobriety*
Tatsache, -n	– _____
Fähigkeit	– _____
zusammenschauend	– *viewing everything as a whole (lit. viewing together)*
wagemutig	– *daring, bold*
Betrachtung	– *contemplation, way of looking at (something)*
wichtig	– _____
vielleicht	– *perhaps*
nimmt (nehmen)	– _____
von ihm	– *from him, of him*
Ausgang	– *starting point*

Task 5:
Read lines 1–12 of the text and answer the questions.

a What does the author think of *von Humboldt's* research work in America?

b Which two qualities of character are ascribed by the author to *von Humboldt*?

c In which fields has *von Humboldt* become an exemplary figure?

d What were *von Humboldt's* achievements in the field of plant geography?

Task 6:
Compare the following statements with the text and select one of the following alternatives:

a This statement appears as such in the text or in other words. Indicate the relevant part of the text.

b This statement does not appear in the text and/or it contradicts the text. What does the text actually have to say on this point?

1 *Alexander von Humboldt* discovered a second route to America.

2 As a scientist he was both sober and imaginative.

3 He developed a new way of describing nature.

4 He indicated a new direction for plant geography.

5 The Spanish-Americans regard him as the indirect founder of their states which were to later emerge.

6 His journey to America was a scientific success.

7 *Bonpland* left his home country, Cuba, together with *Alexander von Humboldt*.

8 Cuba was the last stop on *von Humboldt's* American journey.

Grammar

1 Adjectives as nouns

Adjectives sometimes appear as nouns; they are then capitalized (cf. *Adjectives as Nouns*, pp. 61–62).

möglich angehörig einzigartig
possible belonging (to) unique

Aber der Gedanke überschreitet das soziologisch *Mögliche* . . .
However, the thought transcends the sociologically possible . . .

. . . mehrere *Angehörige* einer Familie . . .
. . . several members of a family . . .

Die „zweite Entdeckung Amerikas" war etwas *Einzigartiges* . . .
The "second discovery of America" was something special . . .

2 Present participle

The present participle consists of the infinitive form with the added ending *-d* (cf. *Present Participle*, p. 91).

einführend herrschend   zusammenschauend
introducing ruling, dominating   viewing everything as a whole

ein einführendes Essay
an introductory essay

herrschende Gruppen
dominant groups

die Fähigkeit zusammenschauender Phantasie
the talent of an imagination which viewed everything as a whole

The present participle also occurs as a noun:

reisend – ein Reisender
travelling – a traveller

Abenteuer eines Weltreisenden
Adventures of a Great Traveller (lit. *world traveller*)

der erste Forschungsreisende
the first explorer (lit. *research traveller*)

3 Personal pronouns *er, sie, es, ihn, ihm*

The personal pronouns *er, sie, es* agree with the gender of the noun and have case forms like the articles *der, die, das* (cf. *Personal Pronouns*, pp. 32–33).

das Gefüge *(structure)*:
Es wurde umgeformt.
It was transformed.

die Tiere *(animals)*:
. . . Signale, für deren Empfang *sie* Sinnesorgane haben.
. . . signals for the reception of which they are equipped with sensory organs.

die Sinnesreize *(sense stimuli)*:
Sie kommen beim Empfänger an.
They arrive at the receiver.

der Kreis *(circle)*:
. . . erscheint der innere Kreis viel größer, wenn *er* im Mittelpunkt kleiner Kreise steht, als wenn größere *ihn* umgeben.
. . . the inner circle appears much bigger if it is at the centre of small circles, than if it is surrounded by bigger ones (lit. *if bigger ones surround it*).

Alexander von Humboldt:
Er ist der erste Forschungsreisende . . .
He is the first explorer . . .

Eine Reihe von Einzelwissenschaften nimmt von *ihm* ihren Ausgang.
A number of individual sciences owe their development to him (lit. *take their beginning from him*).

4 Conjunction *um zu*

The conjunction *um* followed by *zu* + infinitive corresponds to *in order to* (cf. *List of Common Conjunctions*, p. 108). The preposition *zu* appears in verbs with separable prefixes between the prefix and the verb stem (cf. *Infinitive: Use*, p. 86).

. . . verläßt er die Insel Kuba, *um* über Nordamerika nach Europa zurück*zu*kehren.
. . . he leaves the island of Cuba in order to return to Europe via North America.

5 *werden* as a full verb

(See also *Verbs: "werden"*, p. 75).

So *ist* er der Vater einer . . . *geworden*.
Thus he has become the father of . . .

Word formation

1 Suffix -kunde

The noun *Kunde* corresponds to *news, tidings*. Used as a suffix it corresponds to *science of . . .*:

Meereskunde	– *oceanography*	(Meer	– *sea, ocean*)
Länderkunde	– *geography*	(Länder	– *countries*)
Heilkunde	– *medicine*	(heilen	– *to heal*)
Völkerkunde	– *ethnology*	(Völker	– *peoples*)

2 Suffix -artig

The suffix *-artig* is derived from the noun *Art* (*kind, way, manner*) (cf. *Suffixes in Adjectives,* p. 136).

einzigartig	– *unique*	(einzig	– *only, sole, single*)

3 Basic word geben

geben, gab, gegeben	– *to give, gave, given*
es gibt	– *there is/there are*
herausgeben	– *to edit*
ergeben	– *to yield, produce*
sich ergeben	– *to result, turn out*
Ergebnis	– *result, outcome*
Aufgabe	– *task, responsibility*
Begabung	– *talent, gift*
Gabe	– *gift*

4 Prefix Einzel-

The prefix *Einzel-* is derived from the adjective *einzeln (individual, separate, single)* (cf. *Prefixes,* p. 126).

eine Reihe von Einzelwissenschaften
a number of individual sciences

15

Text

Text: A passage from an essay by the physicist *Hermann Bondi* about the limits of research in physics. In this passage *Bondi* summarizes a description of scientific procedure formulated by the philosopher *Karl R. Popper.*

Quelle: Hermann Bondi, Die Grenzen der physikalischen Forschung. In: Grenzen der Erkenntnis, hrsg. von L. Reinisch, Herder Bücherei, Band 357, Freiburg 1969, S. 36.

1 **Theorienbildung**

Eine Aufgabe des Wissenschaftlers ist die Theorienbildung. Eine solche Theorie muß das Wissen ihrer Zeit umfassen und darüber hinaus Voraussagen machen darüber, was zukünftige

5 Beobachtungen und Versuche zeigen sollen. Eine solche Theorienbildung ist ein nicht kalt rationaler, sondern ein imaginationsreicher Vorgang. Er läßt sich nicht mechanisieren, er hängt vom Einfallsreichtum des Wissenschaftlers ab. Wenn die Voraussagen einer neuen Theorie durch Versuche

10 und Beobachtungen bestätigt werden, darf man deshalb nicht sagen, daß die Theorie bewiesen worden sei. Wir müssen dann lediglich von dieser Theorie verlangen, daß sie zu weiteren Aussagen führt. Andererseits kann eine Theorie klarerweise durch Versuche widerlegt werden. Wenn der Ausgang

15 des Versuches im Widerspruch mit den Voraussagen der Theorie ist, dann wissen wir eben, daß diese Theorie falsch ist. Nur solange eine Theorie „gefährlich" lebt, so daß ihr empirisch widersprochen werden kann, ist sie eine wissenschaftliche Theorie. Eine Theorie, so könnte man mit Popper

20 resümieren, kann nie als bewiesen angesehen werden, kann aber jederzeit durch Versuche als falsch gezeigt werden.

Task 1:
Listen and follow the text.
Underline the two nouns occurring most frequently.

Task 2:
Answer the questions.

a What do theory and experiment have to do with each other?
b Why are experiments carried out after a theory has been formulated?
c How can a theory be disproved?

Task 3:
Find the four negatives in the text and put circles around them.

Task 4:
Find the German equivalents in the text and underline them.

a *not a coldly rational, but an imaginative process*
b *it cannot be mechanized*
c *it depends on the scientist's powers of imagination*
d *one may not say that the theory has been proved*
e *then we simply know that this theory is false*
f *a theory can never be regarded as (having been) proved*

Task 5:
Find the four pairs of antonyms in the text and write them on the right.

a *rational* ↔ *imaginative* _____

b *corroborated* ↔ *contradicted* _____

c *proved* ↔ *disproved* _____

d *never* ↔ *at any time* _____

Eine Aufgabe des Wissenschaftlers ist die Theorienbildung. Eine solche Theorie muß das Wissen ihrer Zeit umfassen und darüber hinaus Voraussagen machen darüber, was zukünftige Beobachtungen und Versuche zeigen sollen. Eine solche 5 Theorienbildung ist ein nicht kalt rationaler, sondern ein imaginationsreicher Vorgang. Er läßt sich nicht mechanisieren, er hängt vom Einfallsreichtum des Wissenschaftlers ab.

Task 6:
Read the first part of the text once again; then consult the *Basic Word List* on

Aufgabe – _____

Beobachtungen – _____

Voraussagen – _____

darüber hinaus – _____

zukünftige – _____

(adjective derived from *Zukunft*)

Task 7:
Answer the questions on the first part of the text.

a What is one of the tasks of the scientist?
b What must a theory include?
c About what must a theory make predictions?
d What prior condition must a scientist satisfy in order to be able to construct theories?
e To what word does *ihrer* in front of *Zeit* (line 3) refer?
f To what word does *er* (line 7) refer?

72

10 Wenn die Vorausssagen einer neuen Theorie durch Versuche und Beobachtungen bestätigt werden, darf man deshalb nicht sagen, daß die Theorie bewiesen worden sei. Wir müssen dann lediglich von dieser Theorie verlangen, daß sie zu weiteren Aussagen führt. Andererseits kann eine Theorie klarerweise durch Versuche widerlegt werden. Wenn der Ausgang
15 des Versuches im Widerspruch mit den Voraussagen der Theorie ist, dann wissen wir eben, daß diese Theorie falsch ist.

Task 8:
Read the second part of the text once again; then consult the *Basic Word List* on

andererseits – _____

Ausgang – _____

Aussagen – _____

verlangen – _____

Widerspruch – _____

Task 9:
Answer the questions on the second part of the text.

a How can the predictions of a theory be confirmed?
b How can a theory be clearly refuted?
c When do we know that a theory is false?

Task 10:
Find the two *if – then* sequences in the second part of the text and underline them.

lediglich – *merely;*   weitere – *further;*   klarerweise – *clearly;*
eben – *just, simply*

Nur solange eine Theorie „gefährlich" lebt, so daß ihr empirisch widersprochen werden kann, ist sie eine wissenschaftliche Theorie. Eine Theorie, so könnte man mit Popper resümieren, kann nie als bewiesen angesehen werden, kann 20 aber jederzeit durch Versuche als falsch gezeigt werden.

Task 11:
Read the third part of the text once again; then consult the *Basic Word List* on

gefährlich – _____

solange – _____

zeigen – _____

Task 12:
Answer the questions on the last part of the text.

a How does a theory live *gefährlich*?
b To what word does *ihr* (line 17) refer? In other words: What can be contradicted?
c How could one summarize *Popper*'s thoughts (according to the text)?

Grammar

1 Passive voice

The passive voice is expressed by *werden* + a past participle (cf. *Passive Voice*, p. 93)

Wie kommt es, daß eine bestimmte Sache so und nicht anders *benannt wird*?
How is it that a certain thing is called *this and not something else?*

Eine Theorie kann nie als bewiesen *angesehen werden.*
A theory can never be regarded *as (having been) proved.*

. . . darf man deshalb nicht sagen, daß die Theorie *bewiesen worden sei.**
. . . *one may not say for that reason that the theory* has been proved.

The agent of the action appears with the preposition *durch* (*by*):

Wenn die Voraussagen *durch* Versuche und Beobachtungen *bestätigt werden,* . . .
If the predictions are corroborated by *experiments and observations,* . . .

Andererseits kann eine Theorie *durch* Versuche *widerlegt werden.*
On the other hand a theory can be disproved by *experiments.*

Das starre Gefüge *wurde durch* die politische Demokratisierung *umgeformt.*
The rigid system was transformed by *political democratization.*

2 Modal auxiliaries

Eine solche Theorie *muß* das Wissen ihrer Zeit umfassen.
Such a theory must *comprise the knowledge of its time.*

Wir *müssen* dann lediglich von dieser Theorie verlangen, . . .
We must, *in that case, merely demand of this theory* . . .

. . . *darf* man *nicht* sagen, daß . . .
. . . *one* may not *say that* . . .

. . . Vorraussagen darüber, was zukünftige Beobachtungen und Versuche zeigen *sollen.*
. . . *predictions about what future observations and experiments* are to *show.*

*sei, a subjunctive form, is used here (instead of *ist*) to emphasize that the author considers what others are saying to be incorrect – in his words (preceding the *sei*): *Man darf nicht sagen* . . . (cf. *Reported Speech*, p. 97).

Eine Theorie *kann* jederzeit durch Versuche als falsch gezeigt werden.
A theory can *at any time be shown to be false.*

. . . so *könnte* man mit Popper resümieren . . .
. . . thus we could summarize with Popper . . .

(See also *Modal Auxiliaries*, pp. 77–82).

3 Conjunction *wenn, dann*

Subordinate clauses introduced by *wenn (if)* are sometimes followed by *dann (then)* in the main clause (cf. *List of Common Conjunctions*, p. 108).

Wenn der Ausgang des Versuches im Widerspruch mit den Voraussagen der Theorie ist, *dann* wissen wir eben, daß diese Theorie falsch ist.
If *the outcome of the experiment contradicts the predictions of the theory*, then *we simply know that this theory is false.*

4 Adverb *darüber*

Da- or *dar-* combined with a preposition sometimes precedes a dependent clause (cf. *Da-compounds*, p. 41).

Eine solche Theorie muß Voraussagen machen *darüber, was* zukünftige Beobachtungen und Versuche zeigen sollen.
Such a theory must make predictions about what future observations and experiments shall show.

Word formation

1 Prefix *wider-*

The prefix *wider- (counter-, contra-, against, re-)* comes from the preposition *wider (against).*

widerlegen	from: legen
to disprove, to refute	*to lay, to put*
widersprechen	from: sprechen
to contradict	*to speak*
Widerspruch	noun derived from the verb
contradiction, opposition	

2 Suffix *-reich*

The suffix *-reich (rich in, full of)* comes from the adjective *reich (rich).*

imaginationsreich
full of imagination, imaginative

The noun *der Reichtum (wealth)* is derived from *reich.*

der Einfallsreichtum	from: der Einfall
wealth of ideas, imaginativeness	*idea*

3 Suffix *-seits*

The suffix *-seits (on . . . side)* comes from the noun *die Seite (side)* and is found in adverbs.

andererseits	from: andere
on the other hand	*other*

andererseits is sometimes preceded by *einerseits (on the one hand).*

4 Suffix *-weise*

The suffix *-weise (by way of . . ., -wise, -ly)* comes from the noun *die Weise (way, manner)* and is found in adverbs.

klarerweise	from: klar
clearly	*clear*

Text

Text: This text is a direct continuation of the one in chapter 15 on *Theorienbildung*.

Quelle: Siehe Kapitel 15.

Suggestion: Read the text in chapter 15 once again before starting on this text.

---

1 ## Theorienbildung (2)

Diese, wie mir scheint, ausgezeichnete Beschreibung des wissenschaftlichen Vorgangs läßt sich an vielen Beispielen verdeutlichen. So wurde die Newtonsche Theorie des Schwe-
5 refeldes jahrhundertelang benutzt, um Voraussagen über den genauen Zeitpunkt von Sonnen- und Mondfinsternissen zu machen. Jahrhundertelang schienen die Voraussagen durch die beobachteten Finsternisse bestätigt zu werden. Aber als sich bei der immer größeren Genauigkeit der Untersuchun-
10 gen zwischen Voraussage und Beobachtung Unterschiede zeigten, wurde diese Theorie trotz all der guten Ergebnisse schließlich als widerlegt angesehen. Was für diesen Fall gilt, gilt prinzipiell für jede Theorie, sie kann nie als durch Über-
prüfung bewiesen, nie als endgültig angesehen werden. Alle
15 wissenschaftlichen Theorien sind nur provisorisch.
Es wird gelegentlich gesagt, daß die Wissenschaften und die Theorien uns eine Annäherung an die Wahrheit geben. Ich halte eine solche Aussage deshalb für nicht gut, weil die Wahrheit ein starrer Begriff ist und ich keinen Grund für die
20 Annahme sehe, daß es so etwas Starres in oder hinter der Wissenschaft gebe. Die Geschichte der Naturwissenschaft zeigt, daß ihre Theorien immer wieder durch Methoden und Versuche widerlegt worden sind, die man bis dahin einfach deshalb nicht voraussagen konnte, weil unser Einfallsreich-
25 tum so schwach ist.
. . .

Task 1:
Listen and follow the text. Find out how the text is constructed by giving the numbers of the lines where you can find the following details.

Line(s)

—— a concrete example of the scientific procedure

—— centuries of validity of a particular theory

—— a change in opinion about this theory

—— a general conclusion about theories

—— an impersonal statement about sciences and theories

—— the author's opinion about this anonymous statement

—— a justification of this opinion

—— a reference to history

—— a human weakness on the part of scientists

Task 2:
Check whether you can understand the parts of the text not underlaid in grey. These words and forms have occurred in the preceding chapters.

Task 3:
Read the first part (lines 1–15) of the text once again.

ausgezeichnet – *excellent;* Finsternis,-se – *eclipse;*
Mond – *moon;* Schwerefeld – *field of gravity*

Task 4:
Find the German equivalents in the text and underline them.

a *the theory was used to make predictions*
b *. . . seemed to be corroborated by the observed eclipses*
c *this theory was in the end regarded as (having been) disproved*
d *it can never be regarded as conclusive*

Task 5:
Find the German equivalents in the text and write them on the right. The order of the passages in English does not follow that of the German text.

a *what is valid in this case*

_____

b *in spite of all the good results*

_____

c *can be clarified by means of many examples*

_____

d *when differences became apparent*

_____

e *proved by checking*

_____

f *with the increasingly greater precision of the investigations*

_____

g *as it seems to me*

_____

h *predictions about the exact date*

_____

Theorienbildung (2)

Diese, wie mir scheint, ausgezeichnete Beschreibung des wissenschaftlichen Vorgangs läßt sich an vielen Beispielen verdeutlichen. so wurde die Newtonsche Theorie des Schwe-
5 refeldes jahrhundertelang benutzt, um Voraussagen über den genauen Zeitpunkt von Sonnen- und Mondfinsternissen zu machen. Jahrhundertelang schienen die Voraussagen durch die beobachteten Finsternisse bestätigt zu werden. Aber als sich bei der immer größeren Genauigkeit der Untersuchun-
10 gen zwischen Voraussage und Beobachtung Unterschiede zeigten, wurde diese Theorie trotz all der guten Ergebnisse schließlich als widerlegt angesehen. Was für diesen Fall gilt, gilt prinzipiell für jede Theorie, sie kann nie als durch Über-prüfung bewiesen, nie als endgültig angesehen werden. Alle
15 wissenschaftlichen Theorien sind nur provisorisch.
Es wird gelegentlich gesagt, daß die Wissenschaften und die Theorien uns eine Annäherung an die Wahrheit geben. Ich halte eine solche Aussage deshalb für nicht gut, weil die Wahrheit ein starrer Begriff ist und ich keinen Grund für die
20 Annahme sehe, daß es so etwas Starres in oder hinter der Wissenschaft gebe*. Die Geschichte der Naturwissenschaft zeigt, daß ihre Theorien immer wieder durch Methoden und Versuche widerlegt worden sind, die man bis dahin einfach deshalb nicht voraussagen konnte, weil unser Einfallsreich-
25 tum so schwach ist.
. . .

Task 6:
Answer the questions on the first part of the text.

a How many examples are given in the text?
b In what way was *Newton's* theory of the field of gravity useful for centuries?
c What led to the realization that this theory was not correct?
d In what way is this case exemplary?

Task 7:
Consult the *Basic Word List* on the words written below, then find them in the second part of the text (lines 16–25) and underline them.

Wahrheit   – _____

Begriff   – _____

Annahme   – _____

kein   – _____

*gebe, a subjunctive form, appears here (instead of *gibt*) to emphasize that the author is quoting an assumption which he considers to be groundless. He says (preceding the *gebe*), *ich sehe keinen Grund für die Annahme . . .* (cf. *Reported Speech*, p. 97).

Task 8:
Find the German equivalents in the text and write them on the right.

a *that its theories have been disproved again and again*

_____

b *that there is anything as rigid (as that) in or behind science*

_____

_____

c *it is said occasionally*

_____

d *methods and experiments which we, up to then, simply could not predict*

_____

_____

e *that the sciences give us an approximation of reality*

_____

f *because our imagination is so weak*

_____

g *I consider a statement like this to be not good*

_____

Task 9:
Answer the questions on the second part of the text.

a What does the author think about truth in science?
b What has lack of ingenuity (on the part of the scientists) prevented from happening?
c Where can we find proof that there is nothing rigid in science?

Task 10:
Read the whole text through once again and reproduce the contents in your own words.

Grammar

1 Negatives

nicht
Warum nicht ich?
Why not me?

. . . hinter nicht realisierbaren politischen Versprechungen
. . . *behind unrealizable political promises*

ein nicht kalt rationaler, sondern ein imaginationsreicher Vorgang
not a coldly rational, but an imaginative process

nicht mehr
Das starre Gefüge existiert nicht mehr
The rigid system no longer exists

nicht nur – sondern auch
Das Bevölkerungsbild Europas ist nicht nur das Ergebnis einer natürlichen Entwicklung, sondern auch die Folge großer Wanderungsbewegungen
The distribution of peoples in Europe is not only the result of a natural development, but also the consequence of great migratory movements.

nichts
Viel Lärm um Nichts
Much Ado About Nothing

nie
Eine Theorie kann nie als endgültig angesehen werden.
A theory can never be regarded as conclusive.

kein
. . . weil ich keinen Grund für die Annahme sehe, daß . . .
. . . *because I see no grounds for the assumption that . . .*

weder – noch
Weder haben alle die gleichen Chancen noch die gleichen Kräfte.
Neither do all individuals have the same opportunities nor do they have the same strength.

2 Verb *zeigen*

zeigen appears in chapters 15 and 16 in the active voice, in the passive voice and as a reflexive verb:

Die Geschichte der Naturwissenschaft *zeigt,* daß . . .
The history of natural science shows *that . . .*

. . . was zukünftige Beobachtungen und Versuche *zeigen* sollen.
. . . *what future observations and experiments are to show.*

Eine Theorie kann durch Versuche als falsch *gezeigt werden.*
A theory can be shown *to be false by experiments.*

Als *sich* zwischen Voraussage und Beobachtung Unterschiede *zeigten* . . .
When differences became apparent *between prediction and observation . . .*

3 Verb *lassen*

lassen appears in chapters 15 and 16 with *sich* and a verb in the infinitive:

. . . ein imaginationsreicher Vorgang. Er *läßt sich* nicht *mechanisieren.*
. . . *an imaginative process. It* cannot *be mechanized.*

Diese Beschreibung des wissenschaftlichen Vorgangs *läßt sich* an vielen Beispielen *verdeutlichen.*
This description of the scientific process can be clarified *by means of many examples.*

4 Verb *halten*

halten appears in chapters 13 and 16 in two different meanings:

Alle Varianten *halten sich* streng *an* das Modell . . .
All variants adhere *strictly to the model . . .*

Ich *halte* eine solche Aussage *für* nicht gut.
I consider *a statement like this to be not good.*

5 Adverb *immer*

Immer (always) appears with comparatives of adjectives and with the adverb *wieder:*
Immer mehr Schüler, Eltern und Lehrer . . .
More and more *schoolchildren, parents and teachers . . .*

. . . bei der *immer größeren* Genauigkeit der Untersuchungen . . .
. . . *with the* greater and greater *precision of the investigations . . .*

. . . daß ihre Theorien *immer wieder* widerlegt worden sind.
. . . *that its theories were disproved* again and again.

6 Adverb *deshalb*

Wenn die Voraussagen bestätigt werden, darf man *deshalb* nicht sagen, daß die Theorie bewiesen worden sei.
If the predictions are corroborated, one may not say for this reason *that the theory has been proved.*

Ich halte eine solche Aussage *deshalb* für nicht gut, *weil* die Wahrheit ein starrer Begriff ist und . . .
I consider a statement like this to be not good for the reason that *truth is a rigid concept and . . .*

. . . durch Methoden und Versuche, die man bis dahin einfach *deshalb* nicht voraussagen konnte, *weil* unser Einfallsreichtum so schwach ist.
. . . *by methods and experiments which we could not predict up to then* for the *simple* reason that *our powers of imagination are so poor.*

Word formation

1 Suffix -nis

The suffix -nis appears in nouns derived from verbs or adjectives (cf. *Suffixes in Nouns*, p. 143).

kennen	– *to know*	Kenntnis	– *knowledge*
ergeben	– *to yield*	Ergebnis	– *result, outcome*
finster	– *dark*	Finsternis	– *darkness, eclipse*

2 Nouns derived from verbs

versuchen	– *to try*	Versuch	– *experiment*
vorgehen	– *to proceed*	Vorgang	– *process*
unterscheiden	– *to distinguish*	Unterschied	– *difference*

A large number of these nouns end in *-e* and are feminine in gender:

geben	– *to give*	Gabe	– *gift*
aufgeben	– *to assign*	Aufgabe	– *task, job*
voraussagen	– *to predict*	Voraussage	– *prediction*
aussagen	– *to state*	Aussage	– *statement*
annehmen	– *to assume*	Annahme	– *assumption*
sprechen	– *to speak*	Sprache	– *language*
folgen	– *to follow*	Folge	– *consequence*

3 Deceptive word *prinzipiell*

Was für diesen Fall gilt, gilt prinzipiell für jede Theorie.
What is true of this case is true in principle of every theory.

(Not to be read as *principally* which would be *in erster Linie*.)

Text

Text: Comments about some research techniques, from a chapter on the problem of inductive reasoning.

Quelle: Helmut Seiffert, Einführung in die Wissenschaftstheorie, Bd. 1, Verlag C. H. Beck, München 1971, S. 160–161.

Das Problem des Induktionsschlusses

I. Die Schritte der Forschung

1. Die Forschungstechniken

Die ursprünglichste Technik der Erfahrungswissenschaft ist die *Beobachtung*. Zunächst nämlich beobachtet der forschende Mensch in der Regel etwas, was ohne sein Zutun vor sich geht. Der Musterschauplatz für die Technik der Beobachtung ist natürlich wieder die Astronomie. Denn der Mensch kann Vorgänge am Himmel nicht herbeiführen oder beeinflussen (wenn wir von der Existenz der Raketen, künstlichen Satelliten usw. hier einmal absehen), sondern er kann sie nur wahrnehmen, wie sie sich ohne sein Zutun vollziehen – eben „beobachten".

Aber auch der Sozialwissenschaftler ist weitgehend auf Beobachtungen von Vorgängen angewiesen, die er nicht selbst herbeiführen kann. Anders ist es in der Physik, der Chemie, den anderen Naturwissenschaften und manchmal auch in den Sozialwissenschaften. Hier kann der Forscher Vorgänge, die er beobachten will, um allgemeine Gesetzmäßigkeiten zu finden, selber herbeiführen. Dieses Herbeiführen nennen wir *Experiment*.

Auch in den Sozialwissenschaften kommt das Experiment gelegentlich vor. Hier tritt es auch in Sonderformen mit eigener Bezeichnung auf, zum Beispiel „Test" (vor allem in der Psychologie) oder „Befragung" (vor allem in der Sozialforschung).

Alle empirischen Forschungstechniken, wie Beobachtung, Experiment, Test und Befragung, stellen besondere methodische Probleme, die in einer eigenen Methodenlehre bearbeitet werden müssen.

Da vor allem Beobachtungen, Experimente und Tests, aber auch Befragungen es oft mit quantitativen Größen zu tun haben, die exakt erfaßt werden müssen, ist die Lehre vom *Messen* ein zentraler Bereich der empirischen Methodenlehre.

(Zeilennummern: 1, 5, 10, 15, 20, 25, 30, 35)

Task 1:
Listen and follow the text, then read the text once again and answer the questions.

a How many research techniques can you find in the text? (Underline them.)
b Which is the earliest research technique?
c Which science is the exemplary field for this technique?
d What role is played by human beings in this science?
e In which sciences is the human being himself able to bring about certain events for his own purpose?
f What names are given to certain experiments in the social sciences? (Underline the terms.)
g Which method is, to your knowledge, employed in social research? In other words, what does *Befragung* probably mean?
h What name is given to the science which is concerned with methodological problems? (Underline the term.)
i What technique or method is concerned with quantities? In other words, what does *Messen* probably mean?
j Where does the text say something about the difference between observation and experiment? Give the numbers of the lines.
k Where does the text say something general about research techniques? Give the numbers of the lines.

Task 2:
Complete the following statements by quoting from the text.

a Beobachtung, _____ und _____ sind empirische Forschungstechniken.

b Die Beobachtung ist eine _____. Experiment und Messen sind auch _____ _____.

c Naturwissenschaften und _____ sind empirische Wissenschaften.

d Physik und Chemie sind _____. Die Psychologie ist eine der _____.

e Der Test ist eine Form von _____ in der _____. Die Befragung ist eine andere Form von _____ in der _____.

f Der Astronom kann Vorgänge nicht selbst _____, sondern nur _____. Ein Physiker oder Chemiker kann Vorgänge, die er beobachten will, selbst _____.

1. Die Forschungstechniken

Die ursprünglichste Technik der Erfahrungswissenschaft
5 ist die *Beobachtung*. Zunächst nämlich beobachtet der forschende Mensch in der Regel etwas, was ohne sein Zutun vor
sich geht. Der Musterschauplatz für die Technik der Beobachtung ist natürlich wieder die Astronomie. Denn der
Mensch kann Vorgänge am Himmel nicht herbeiführen oder
10 beeinflussen (wenn wir von der Existenz der Raketen, künstlichen Satelliten usw. hier einmal absehen), sondern er kann
sie nur wahrnehmen, wie sie sich ohne sein Zutun vollziehen –
eben „beobachten".

Aber auch der Sozialwissenschaftler ist weitgehend auf
15 Beobachtungen von Vorgängen angewiesen, die er nicht
selbst herbeiführen kann. Anders ist es in der Physik, der
Chemie, den anderen Naturwissenschaften und manchmal
auch in den Sozialwissenschaften. Hier kann der Forscher
Vorgänge, die er beobachten will, um allgemeine Gesetzmä-
20 ßigkeiten zu finden, selber herbeiführen. Dieses Herbeiführen nennen wir *Experiment*.

Auch in den Sozialwissenschaften kommt das Experiment
gelegentlich vor. Hier tritt es auch in Sonderformen mit
eigener Bezeichnung auf, zum Beispiel „Test" (vor allem in
25 der Psychologie) oder „Befragung" (vor allem in der Sozialforschung).

Alle empirischen Forschungstechniken, wie Beobachtung,
Experiment, Test und Befragung, stellen besondere methodische Probleme, die in einer eigenen Methodenlehre bearbei-
30 tet werden müssen.

Da vor allem Beobachtungen, Experimente und Tests,
aber auch Befragungen es oft mit quantitativen Größen zu tun
haben, die exakt erfaßt werden müssen, ist die Lehre vom
Messen ein zentraler Bereich der empirischen Methoden-
35 lehre.

Task 3:
Quote from the text the nouns to which the pronouns refer.

Line

6   sein: _____

11   er: _____

12   sie: _____

12   sie: _____

15   die: _____

15   er: _____

19   die: _____

19   er: _____

23   es: _____

29   die: _____

33   die: _____

Task 4:
Find the German equivalents in the text and underline them.

a   *the first and earliest tech-*   e   *with separate designations*
   nique   f   *with quantifiable dimen-*
b   *without his assistance*   *sions*
c   *artificial satellites*   g   *a central area*
d   *general laws of nature*

Task 5:
Quote synonymous expressions from the text. – If necessary,
consult the *Basic Word List* on the words set in italics.

a   Die *erste Methode* in der *empirischen Wissenschaft* ist die
   Beobachtung.

   Die _____ _____ in der

   _____ ist die Beobachtung.

b   Der Astronom kann Vorgänge am Himmel nur *wahrnehmen*.

   Er kann sie nur _____ .

c   . . . was *sich* ohne sein Zutun *vollzieht*.

   . . . was ohne sein Zutun _____ _____ _____ .

d   Auch in den Sozialwissenschaften *tritt* das Experiment
   manchmal auf.

   Auch in den Sozialwissenschaften _____ das Experiment

   _____ _____ .

e   Test und Befragung sind *besondere Arten* des Experiments.

   Test und Befragung sind _____

   des Experiments.

Schritt, -e	– *step*		eben (adverb)	– *just, simply; exactly*
Muster- (in compounds)	– *model, classic, exemplary*		vor allem	– *above all*
Schauplatz	– *scene, setting*		da (conjunction)	– *as, since*
Himmel	– *sky, heavens*			

Task 6:
Find the German equivalents in the text and write them on the left.

a _____ *something which happens*

b _____ *if we, for now, disregard the existence of rockets*

c _____ *he can perceive them happening*

d _____ *. . . is largely dependent on observations*

e _____ *. . . which must be worked on in a particular methodology*

f _____ *. . . which must be recorded exactly*

Task 7:
Read the text once again and answer the questions.

a Why is astronomy a fine example of the technique of observation?
b Why is it that experiments are only occasionally performed in the social sciences? – No reason is given in the text. What do you suppose might be the reason?

c Why is it necessary to have a special theory of method?
d Why does the theory of measurement play such a central role in empirical methodology?

Grammar

1 Conjunction *da*

da introduces subordinate clauses. It corresponds to *since, as, seeing that* (cf. *List of Common Conjunctions*, p. 105).

Da vor allem Beobachtungen . . . es oft mit quantitativen Größen zu tun haben, ist die Lehre vom Messen ein zentraler Bereich der empirischen Methodenlehre.
Since observations . . . above all often involve quantitative entities, the theory of measurement is central to the empirical theory of method.

2 Relative pronoun *was*

was occurs as a relative pronoun referring to *etwas* (cf. *Relative Pronouns*, pp. 39–40).

. . . etwas, was ohne sein Zutun vor sich geht.
. . . something which happens without his assistance.

3 Preposition *ohne*

. . . ohne sein Zutun . . .
. . . without his assistance . . .

Word formation

1 Suffix *-mäßig*

The suffix *-mäßig* is derived from the noun *das Maß (measure, extent)* and corresponds to *in the manner of, according to* (cf. *Suffixes in Adjectives*, p. 139).

gesetzmäßig   from: Gesetz
in accordance with a law   *law*

. . . um allgemeine Gesetzmäßigkeiten zu finden . . .
. . . in order to find general laws (or regularities) . . .

2 Prefix *zu-*

The prefix *zu-* occurs in verbs in the sense of *to add* (cf. *Prefixes*, p. 135).

ohne seine Zutun
without his doing anything (without his assistance)

3 Prefix *Sonder-*

The prefix *Sonder-* corresponds to *special, separate* (cf. *Prefixes*, p. 131).

Sonderformen (des Experiments) mit eigener Bezeichnung
special forms (of the experiment) with separate terms

4 *anders/andere*

Anders ist es in der Physik . . .
It is different in physics . . .

. . . weil Alexander anders war als die Menschen seiner Zeit.
. . . because Alexander was different from the people of his time.

Wie jede andere Heilkunde . . .
Like any other form of medicine . . .

. . . in den anderen Naturwissenschaften
. . . in the other natural sciences

5 *besonders/besondere*

. . . spielen eine besonders deutliche Rolle
. . . play a particularly significant role

. . . stellen besondere methodische Probleme
. . . present special methodological problems

6 Derivative *künstlich*

The adjective *künstlich* is derived from the noun *die Kunst (art)*:

künstliche Satelliten
artificial (or *man-made*) *satellites*

Text

Text: The last chapter of the book *Strukturen der Natur* by the natural scientist *Karl-Erik Zimen* entitled *Consequences of Progress: The Change of Life of Humanity* is concerned with the necessity of a change above all in our spiritual attitudes. The chapter suggests that it is an illusion to think that technical progress will go on for ever. Humanity has reached the limits of its growth. The "point of no return" is dangerously near. *Zimen* quotes the opinions of other authors on this topic, among them the German philosopher of religion *Romano Guardini* (1885–1968).

Quelle: Karl-Erik Zimen, Strukturen der Natur, © by Nymphenburger Verlagshandlung GmbH, München.

---

1 **Geistige Übungen für sogenannte Realisten?**

. . . Der Religionsphilosoph R. Guardini hat einmal geäußert: „Wenn man aber doch etwas Konkretes zu sagen versuchte und etwa den Vorschlag machte, Unternehmer wie
5 Ingenieure sollten einmal im Jahre geistige Übungen machen,
d. h. sich irgendwohin zurückziehen, wo es still wäre, wirklich
still; und wo ein Mensch, der das nötige Wissen von den
Fundamenten des Daseins hätte, ihnen etwas über Fragen des
kontemplativen Lebens sagte? Vielleicht würde manch einer,
10 der auf seinen Realismus pocht, über einen solchen Vorschlag
lachen. Ein gescheiter Chinese würde, glaube ich, nicht
lachen. Vielleicht würde er sich sogar wundern, daß wir seit so
langer Zeit mit so explosiven Dingen wie Wissenschaft und
Technik umgehen und noch nicht gemerkt haben, was da
15 passieren kann und *welcher geistigen Voraussetzung es bedarf,
damit nichts passiert.*"

Task 1:
Look at the external form of the text and the punctuation and answer the questions which follow.

a   Where does the quotation begin and where does it end?
b   What seems to be especially important in this text?
c   Which symbol can be found at the end of the sentence beginning with *Wenn* (line 3)? What type of sentence is it?
d   What do you expect to find in the sentences which follow?

Task 2:
Listen and follow the text; read it to yourself and underline all the people who are mentioned.

Task 3:
Discuss amongst yourselves to which of the persons mentioned in the text you would assign the following concepts (and why).

a   das Wissen von den Fundamenten des Daseins (l. 7–8)
b   Fragen des kontemplativen Lebens (l. 8–9)
c   Realismus (l. 10)
d   Wissenschaft und Technik (l. 13–14)

Task 4:
Find the German equivalents in the text and underline them.

a   *if one were perhaps to make the suggestion*
b   *do spiritual exercises once a year*

c   *retreat somewhere where it would be quiet*
d   *perhaps many a man would laugh at such a suggestion*
e   *perhaps he would even be surprised*
f   *what can happen*
g   *what spiritual qualification is necessary*

Task 5:
Check in what context these words occur in the text and supply a suitable English equivalent, from memory, by guesswork or with the help of the *Basic Word List.*

äußern	– _____
versuchen	– _____
Unternehmer	– *entrepreneur, industrialist*
wirklich	– _____
Dasein	– _____
ihnen	– _____
pochen auf	– *to insist on; to make much of*
gescheit	– *clever, sensible, wise*
glauben	– _____
umgehen mit	– *to deal with, to handle*
merken	– *to notice*
noch	– _____
damit	– *in order that, to the end that*

Task 6:
Read the text once again and answer the questions.

a   Who does *Guardini* mean here when he says *man* (line 3)?
b   What would the concrete suggestion be?
c   Why is *Guardini* thinking precisely of *Unternehmer und Ingenieure?*
d   What reaction does he expect from a *Realist?*
e   Why does *Guardini* think that *ein gescheiter Chinese würde nicht lachen?*
f   Who does *Guardini* mean here when he says *wir* (line 12)?
g   How do you understand the word *nichts* in the expression *damit nichts passiert* (line 16)? – What is it that must not happen?

Task 7:
Find all the verbs in the text and underline them. Then try to decide which of them appear in hypothetical statements. – Putting the question more formally: Which of the verbs appear in the subjunctive form?

Grammar

1 Subjunctive II

Guardini speaks of a possible suggestion (*Wenn . . . etwa – If . . . perhaps*) and the possible reactions (*vielleicht – perhaps*). In this context the verbs appear in the subjunctive form (cf. *Subjunctive: Forms*, p. 95, and *Use*, p. 99).

The irregular verbs have unambiguous subjunctive forms:

. . . sich irgendwohin zurückziehen, wo es still *wäre*
. . . *retreat somewhere where it* would be *quiet*

. . . ein Mensch, der das nötige Wissen *hätte*
. . . *someone who* would have *the necessary knowledge*

Ein gescheiter Chinese *würde* nicht lachen. Vielleicht *würde* er sich sogar wundern, daß . . .
A clever Chinese would *not laugh. Perhaps he* would *even be surprised that* . . .

The forms of the regular verbs are ambiguous. They could appear as past tense forms in a text which deals with the past. Here, in the context of *wenn . . . etwa . . . vielleicht* and together with *hätte . . . wäre . . . würde*, they appear as subjunctive forms:

Wenn man aber doch etwas Konkretes zu sagen *versuchte* . . .
If one were, *nevertheless,* to attempt *to say something concrete* . . .

Wenn man . . . etwa den Vorschlag *machte* . . .
If one were . . . *perhaps* to make *the suggestion* . . .

Unternehmer wie Ingenieure *sollten* geistige Übungen machen
entrepreneurs and engineers alike should *do spiritual exercises*

. . . wo ein Mensch . . . ihnen etwas über Fragen des kontemplativen Lebens *sagte*
. . . *where someone* . . . were to tell *them something about questions of contemplative life*

2 Conjunction *damit*

(Cf. *List of Common Conjunctions*, p. 106)

. . . welcher geistigen Voraussetzung es bedarf, damit nichts passiert.
. . . *what spiritual qualification is necessary in order that nothing does happen.*

3 Personal pronouns *sie, ihnen*

(Cf. *Personal Pronouns*, p. 33)

Er kann sie (die Vorgänge am Himmel) nur wahrnehmen.
He can only perceive them.

wo ein Mensch ihnen (den Unternehmern und Ingenieuren) etwas sagte . . .
where someone were to tell them something . . .

4 Various uses of *wie*

Die linke Strecke ist *genauso lang wie* die rechte.
The left-hand line is just as long as *the right-hand one.*

Wie sind die Wörter entstanden?
How *did words originate?*

Ursachen und Anlässe *wie* Klimawandel, Bedrohung . . .
causes and reasons like *change of climate, threats* . . .

Wie jede andere Heilkunde beschäftigte sich auch die Psychotherapie mit . . .
Like *any other form of medicine psychotherapy was also concerned with* . . .

Unternehmer *wie* Ingenieure sollten geistige Übungen machen
entrepreneurs and *engineers* alike *should do spiritual exercises*

Er kann sie (die Vorgänge am Himmel) nur wahrnehmen, *wie* sie sich vollziehen.
*He can only perceive them happen*ing (lit. *as they happen*).

Word formation

1 Prefix *irgend-*

(Cf. *Prefixes*, p. 129)

. . . sich *irgend*wohin zurückziehen, wo es still wäre
. . . *retreat* some*where where it would be quiet*

2 Suffix *-mal*

(Cf. *Suffixes in Adjectives*, p. 139)

Guardini hat *einmal* geäußert . . .
Guardini once *said* . . .

einmal im Jahre
once *a year*

und *manchmal* auch in den Sozialwissenschaften
and sometimes *even in the social sciences*

3 Words which are easily confused: *etwas/etwa*

Wenn man *etwas* Konkretes zu sagen versuchte . . .
If one were to say something *concrete* . . .

Wenn man . . . *etwa* den Vorschlag machte . . .
If one were . . . perhaps *to make the suggestion* . . .

4 Abbreviation *d. h.*

(Cf. *Abbreviations*, p. 189f.)

geistige Übungen machen, *d. h.* sich irgendwohin zurückziehen, wo es still wäre . . .
do spiritual exercises, that is to say retreat somewhere where it would be quiet . . .

Text

Text: One chapter of a handbook on Europe is dedicated to industry and trade. The text is from the section on the beginnings of the Industrial Revolution.

Quelle: W. Sperling/A. Karger (Hrsg.), Fischer Länderkunde Europa, Fischer Taschenbuch, Bd. 6127, Frankfurt 1978, S. 114.

Task 1:
Listen and follow the text. Then put a circle round all those words and expressions which have to do with industry and trade.

Die Industrielle Revolution

1 . . . Die Industrielle Revolution nahm nicht zufällig von England aus ihren Lauf. Daß hier Lage und natürliche Ressourcen zuerst „raumwirksam" gemacht wurden, hatte seine
5 Ursachen in der *Gesellschaft* und in der sozialen Infrastruktur. Der vorangegangene Bevölkerungsanstieg, die relative Ruhe nach den Glaubenskriegen, billige Rohstoffzufuhren durch koloniale Aktivitäten, Kapitalakkumulation in nie gekanntem Maße, neue Formen der Unternehmertätigkeit
10 und der Arbeitsorganisation und das liberale Klima einer rationalen Wirtschaftspolitik wirkten zusammen. Bei früheren Konjunkturen war es im allgemeinen so, daß ein starker Bevölkerungsanstieg gefolgt war, so daß der Gewinn rasch wieder aufgezehrt wurde; jetzt aber stiegen die Wachstumsra-
15 ten der Produktion und des Einkommens schneller an als die Bevölkerung. Die Verbesserung der Lebensbedingungen, der Rückgang der Geburten bei gleichzeitiger Verlängerung des durchschnittlichen Lebensalters und nicht zuletzt ein neuer Lebensstil der bürgerlichen Gesellschaft selbst sorgten
20 dafür, daß das akkumulierte Kapital rascher in den Produktionsprozeß zurückfloß und diesen dadurch beschleunigte . . .

Task 2:
Answer the questions.

a What does *Bevölkerung* mean? (Remember the text on *Geographische Mobilität*, chap. 14.)
b What does *Gesellschaft* mean? (Think of *eine elitäre Gesellschaft*, chap. 10, and *klassenlose Gesellschaft*, chap. 11.)
c What does *bürgerlich* mean in the context *ein neuer Lebensstil der bürgerlichen Gesellschaft* (line 19)?

Task 3:
Find the German equivalents in the text and underline them.

a *the previous* (lit. *before-gone*) *increase in population*
b *the relative peace after the religious wars* (lit. *faith wars*)
c *new forms of capital enterprise* (lit. *of entrepreneur activity*)
d *In previous booms it was generally the case that . . .*
e *so that profits had again quickly been used up* (lit. *the profit was . . . eaten up*)
f *the improvement of living conditions*
g *with a simultaneous increase of average life expectancy* (lit. *lengthening of average life-age*)

Task 4:
Find the German equivalents in the text and write them down.

a *It was not by chance that the industrial revolution started in England* (lit. *took its course from E.*) _____

b *. . . had its roots* (lit. *causes) in the society* _____

c *the accumulation of capital on a previously unknown scale* (lit. *a never known measure/extent*) _____

d *that a sharp increase in population had followed* _____

e *the decrease in the birth rate* (lit. *back-going of births*) _____

f *that accumulated capital flowed back quicker into the production process* _____

1 Die Industrielle Revolution

. . . Die Industrielle Revolution nahm nicht zufällig von England aus ihren Lauf. Daß hier Lage und natürliche Ressourcen zuerst „raumwirksam" gemacht wurden, hatte seine

5 Ursachen in der *Gesellschaft* und in der sozialen Infrastruktur. Der vorangegangene Bevölkerungsanstieg, die relative Ruhe nach den Glaubenskriegen, billige Rohstoffzufuhren durch koloniale Aktivitäten, Kapitalakkumulation in nie gekanntem Maße, neue Formen der Unternehmertätigkeit

10 und der Arbeitsorganisation und das liberale Klima einer rationalen Wirtschaftspolitik wirkten zusammen. Bei früheren Konjunkturen war es im allgemeinen so, daß ein starker Bevölkerungsanstieg gefolgt war, so daß der Gewinn rasch wieder aufgezehrt wurde; jetzt aber stiegen die Wachstumsra-

15 ten der Produktion und des Einkommens schneller an als die Bevölkerung. Die Verbesserung der Lebensbedingungen, der Rückgang der Geburten bei gleichzeitiger Verlängerung des durchschnittlichen Lebensalters und nicht zuletzt ein neuer Lebensstil der bürgerlichen Gesellschaft selbst sorgten

20 dafür, daß das akkumulierte Kapital rascher in den Produktionsprozeß zurückfloß und diesen dadurch beschleunigte . . .

Task 5:
Check in what context the words occur in the text and supply a suitable English equivalent, either from memory, by guesswork or with the help of the *Basic Word List*.

Lage	_____	Wirtschaft	_____
zuerst	_____	zusammen	_____
Raum	_____	jetzt	_____
wirksam	_____	ansteigen	_____
billig	– *cheap*	Wachstum	_____
Zufuhr	– *supply*	schnell	_____

nicht zuletzt	_____	dadurch	_____
dafür sorgen, daß	_____	beschleunigen	_____

Task 6:
With the aid of the context decide which function the ending *-er* has in the following words. In other words: Is it a comparative form or is it a case ending?

a Line 11: früher   d Line 17: gleichzeitiger
b Line 12: starker   e Line 19: neuer
c Line 15: schneller   f Line 20: rascher

Task 7:
Compare the following statements with the text and discuss amongst yourselves to what degree they are in accordance with the text or contradict it.

a Es war kein Zufall, daß die Industrielle Revolution in England begann.
b Mit den natürlichen Ressourcen konnte die soziale Infrastruktur verbessert werden.
c Sieben Faktoren wirkten zusammen.
d Vor der Industriellen Revolution gab es keinen Bevölkerungsanstieg.
e Aus den Kolonien kamen billige Rohstoffe ins Land.
f Das Kapital wurde wie früher akkumuliert.
g Die Arbeit wurde anders als früher organisiert.
h Nach einem Bevölkerungszuwachs folgte in früherer Zeit eine Konjunktur.
i Weil es mehr Menschen gab, wurde der Gewinn schnell aufgezehrt.
j Der Anstieg von Produktion, Einkommen und Bevölkerung war jetzt einander proportional.
k Bessere Lebensbedingungen waren die Ursache für den Geburtenrückgang.
l Im Durchschnitt lebten die Menschen länger als früher.
m Die Geburtenrate ging zurück, weil die Gesellschaft einen neuen Lebensstil hatte.
n Weil das Kapital schneller in den Produktionsprozeß zurückfloß, wurde dieser beschleunigt.

Grammar

1 Preposition *bei*

(Cf. *List of Common Prepositions*, pp. 48–49)

Bei früheren Konjunkturen war es im allgemeinen so, daß . . .
In *previous booms it was generally the case that* . . .

der Rückgang der Geburten *bei* gleichzeitiger Verlängerung des durchschnittlichen Lebensalters . . .
the decrease in the birth rate accompanied by *an increase in average life expectancy* . . .

Bei den Griechen blühten die verschiedenen Dichtungsarten . . .
With *the Greeks (i.e. in Greece) the various literary genres flourished* . . .

Als sich *bei* der immer größeren Genauigkeit der Untersuchungen Unterschiede zeigten . . .
When with the increasingly greater precision of the investigations differences became apparent . . .

Die Signale kommen gleichzeitig *beim* Empfänger an.
The signals arrive at the receiver at the same time.

2 Prepositions

A preposition can occur together with another preposition (cf. *Prepositions*, p. 45).

bis   in:
until (into/in)

bis in die Gegenwart
until the present day

von . . . aus:
from   (out of)

von England aus
from England

3 *da*-compounds

Prepositions often occur written together with *da-* or *dar- (there)* (cf. *Da-compounds*, pp. 41–42).

Sogenannte „natürliche" Ursachen waren nicht die einzigen; *dazu* kamen noch Übervölkerung, Wandel des Lebensstils . . .
So-called "natural" causes were not the only ones; to these (thereto) were added overpopulation, changes in life style . . .

. . . achtete man in der Regel *darauf, daß* jeder für sich seinen eigenen Therapeuten erhielt.
. . . it was generally arranged that each was allocated his own therapist.
(darauf achten, daß – *to take care that*)

. . . Voraussagen *darüber, was* zukünftige Beobachtungen und Versuche zeigen sollen.
. . . predictions about what future observations and experiments are to show.

. . . sorgten *dafür, daß* das akkumulierte Kapital rascher in den Produktionsprozeß zurückfloß und diesen *dadurch* beschleunigte.
. . . ensured that accumulated capital flowed back quicker into the production process and thus (thereby) accelerated it.
(dafür sorgen, daß – *to see to it that*)

4 Dative ending *-e*

Some masculine and neuter nouns (mostly monosyllabic) have the optional ending *-e* in the dative singular (cf. *Nouns: Declension*, pp. 26–27).

einmal im Jahre (also: im Jahr)
once a year

in nie gekanntem Maße (or Maß)
on a previously unknown scale

Word formation

1 Prefixes *Rück-* and *zurück-*
(Cf. *Prefixes*, pp. 131 and 135)

der Rückgang der Geburten
the decrease in the birth rate

Rückseite eines Bronzespiegels
reverse of a bronze mirror

. . . um nach Europa zurückzukehren.
. . . in order to return to Europe.

. . . daß das akkumulierte Kapital zurückfloß
. . . that accumulated capital flowed back

2 Derivatives from adjectives

besser
better

Verbesserung
improvement (betterment)

länger
longer

Verlängerung
prolongation (lengthening)

schleunig
prompt, rapid

beschleunigen
to accelerate

3 Suffix *-tum*
(Cf. *Suffixes in Nouns*, p. 144)

wachsen
to grow

Wachstum
growth

reich
rich

Reichtum
wealth

20

Text

Text: In his work *Philosophical Investigations Ludwig Wittgenstein* recorded his thoughts on various subjects in the form of comments in short paragraphs. In Part 1 of the work these comments are numbered from 1 to 693. A great number of them are concerned with language. The 23rd is concerned with so-called language games. It begins with the question of how many types of sentences there are. The grammarians distinguish only three.

Quelle: Ludwig Wittgenstein, Philosophische Untersuchungen, stw 203, © Suhrkamp Verlag, Frankfurt am Main 1977, S. 28–29.

Task 1:
First read the short biographical note on the author and answer the questions which follow:

> 1 *Ludwig Wittgenstein,* geboren am 26. April 1889 in Wien, gestorben am 29. April 1951 in Cambridge, studierte Philosophie bei *Bertrand Russell* in Cambridge, wo er von 1939 bis 1947 den Lehrstuhl für Philosophie innehatte. Werke: *Tractatus logico-philosophicus, Tagebücher 1914–1916, Philoso-*
> 5 *phische Untersuchungen.* Sammlung seiner Werke in der fünf-bändigen Ausgabe der *Schriften,* Frankfurt 1960 ff.

a When did *Wittgenstein* live?
b Where did he come from?
c Who was his teacher?
d How long did he occupy the chair in Philosophy at Cambridge?
e How many of his works have appeared as individual editions?
f When did a collected edition of his works appear?

Task 2:
Listen and follow the text. Then read it again to yourself and underline the words related to language and to games.

Task 3:
Examine the external form of the text, its typographical lay-out, and answer the questions which follow.

a What can you deduce from the fact that lines 16–33 are indented? – What clue is provided by line 15?
b Why are some expressions (in lines 3, 9, 11 and 38) printed in italics? – Do the italics in line 38 serve the same function as in the other lines?
c What is the function of the inverted commas in lines 5 and 11?

Sprachspiele

1 23. Wieviele Arten der Sätze gibt es aber? Etwa Behauptung, Frage und Befehl? – Es gibt *unzählige* solcher Arten: unzählige verschiedene Arten der Verwendung alles dessen, was wir „Zeichen", „Worte", „Sätze", nennen. Und diese Mannigfal-
5 tigkeit ist nichts Festes, ein für allemal Gegebenes; sondern neue Typen der Sprache, neue Sprachspiele, wie wir sagen können, entstehen und andre veralten und werden vergessen. (Ein *ungefähres Bild* davon können uns die Wandlungen der Mathematik geben.)
10 Das Wort „Sprach*spiel*" soll hier hervorheben, daß das Sprechen der Sprache ein Teil ist einer Tätigkeit, oder einer Lebensform.
Führe dir die Mannigfaltigkeit der Sprachspiele an diesen Beispielen, und anderen, vor Augen:
15 Befehlen, und nach Befehlen handeln –
Beschreiben eines Gegenstands nach dem Ansehen, oder nach Messungen –
Herstellen eines Gegenstands nach einer Beschreibung (Zeichnung) –
20 Berichten eines Hergangs –
Über den Hergang Vermutungen anstellen –
Eine Hypothese aufstellen und prüfen –
Darstellen der Ergebnisse eines Experiments durch Tabellen und Diagramme –
25 Eine Geschichte erfinden; und lesen –
Theater spielen –
Reigen singen –
Rätsel raten –
Einen Witz machen; erzählen –
30 Ein angewandtes Rechenexempel lösen –
Aus einer Sprache in die andere übersetzen –
Bitten, Danken, Fluchen, Grüßen, Beten.
– Es ist interessant, die Mannigfaltigkeit der Werkzeuge der Sprache und ihrer Verwendungsweisen, die Mannigfaltigkeit
35 der Wort- und Satzarten, mit dem zu vergleichen, was Logiker über den Bau der Sprache gesagt haben. (Und auch der Verfasser der *Logisch-Philosophischen Abhandlung.*)

Task 4:
Find the German equivalents in the text and underline them.

a *statement, question and command*
b *countless different kinds of use*
c *symbols, words, sentences*
d *the multiplicity of language games*
e *the multiplicity of the tools in language*
f *the multiplicity of types of word and sentence*

etwa	– *for instance;* in questions also *perhaps*
alles dessen	– *of all that*
ein für allemal	– *once and for all*
veralten	– *to become obsolete*
(from: alt	– *old)*
Bild	– *picture, image*
Wandlung	– *change*

88

Task 5:
Read lines 2–13 of the text once again. Then find the German equivalents in the text and write them on the right.

a *not something fixed*

b *new types of language come into existence*

c *others get forgotten*

d *a rough idea of this*

e *what we call symbols*

f *as we may say*

g *is supposed to emphasize*

h *part of an activity, or of a form of life*

Task 6:
Answer the questions on lines 2–13.

a How many types of sentences are there according to *Wittgenstein*?
b What does *Wittgenstein* have to say about old and new language games?
c What reasons does he give for employing this concept?

Task 7:
Discuss amongst yourselves what you understand by language games before examining the second part of the text more closely to see what examples *Wittgenstein* provides by way of illustration. (Lines 14–33)

führe dir . . . vor Augen   – *imagine*
                                (lit. *bring before your eyes*) . . .

Task 8:
Read lines 14–33 once again. Then find the German equivalents in the text and underline them.

a *asking, thanking, cursing, greeting, praying*
b *play-acting*
c *singing catches*
d *giving orders*
e *obeying orders* (lit. *acting according to orders*)
f *guessing riddles*
g *making a joke*
h *telling a joke*

Task 9:
Find the German equivalents in the text and write them on the right.

a *presenting the results of an experiment*

b *describing the appearance of an object*

c *constructing an object from a description*

d *inventing a story; and reading it*

e *speculating about an event*

f *solving a problem in applied arithmetic*

g *forming and testing a hypothesis*

h *translating*

23. Wieviele Arten der Sätze gibt es aber? Etwa Behauptung, Frage und Befehl? – Es gibt *unzählige* solcher Arten: unzählige verschiedene Arten der Verwendung alles dessen, was wir

5 „Zeichen", „Worte", „Sätze", nennen. Und diese Mannigfaltigkeit ist nichts Festes, ein für allemal Gegebenes; sondern neue Typen der Sprache, neue Sprachspiele, wie wir sagen können, entstehen und andre veralten und werden vergessen. (Ein *ungefähres Bild* davon können uns die Wandlungen der

10 Mathematik geben.)
Das Wort „Sprach*spiel*" soll hier hervorheben, daß das Sprechen der Sprache ein Teil ist einer Tätigkeit, oder einer Lebensform.
Führe dir die Mannigfaltigkeit der Sprachspiele an diesen

15 Beispielen, und anderen, vor Augen:
Befehlen, und nach Befehlen handeln –
Beschreiben eines Gegenstands nach dem Ansehen, oder nach Messungen –
Herstellen eines Gegenstands nach einer Beschreibung

20 (Zeichnung) –
Berichten eines Hergangs –
Über den Hergang Vermutungen anstellen –
Eine Hypothese aufstellen und prüfen –
Darstellen der Ergebnisse eines Experiments durch Tabel-

25 len und Diagramme –
Eine Geschichte erfinden; und lesen –
Theater spielen –
Reigen singen –
Rätsel raten –

30 Einen Witz machen; erzählen –
Ein angewandtes Rechenexempel lösen –
Aus einer Sprache in die andere übersetzen –
Bitten, Danken, Fluchen, Grüßen, Beten.
– Es ist interessant, die Mannigfaltigkeit der Werkzeuge der

35 Sprache und ihrer Verwendungsweisen, die Mannigfaltigkeit der Wort- und Satzarten, mit dem zu vergleichen, was Logiker über den Bau der Sprache gesagt haben. (Und auch der Verfasser der *Logisch-Philosophischen Abhandlung.*)

Task 10:
Read lines 34–38 once again. Then find the German equivalents in the text and write them down.

a *the structure of language*

_____

b *it is interesting to compare*

_____

c *what logicians have said*

_____

d *the multiplicity of the ways they are used* (lit. *of their ways of use*)

_____

Task 11:
Look at the whole text once again and discuss the following questions.

a Who is *Wittgenstein* referring to when he says *wir* and *uns* (in lines 2–10)?
b To whom does he say *führe dir vor Augen* (lines 14–15)?
c To whom does he address the questions at the beginning (lines 2–3)?
d To whom is he referring at the end? Who is *der Verfasser der Logisch-Philosophischen Abhandlung* (lines 36–38)?

Grammar

1 Demonstrative pronoun *das/dem/dessen*

A dependent clause introduced by *was (what/which)* is sometimes preceded by the demonstrative pronoun *das/dem/dessen* (cf. *Pronouns*, pp. 37–38).

verschiedene Arten der Verwendung alles *dessen, was* wir Zeichen, Worte, Sätze nennen
different kinds of use of what (lit. *of all that which*) *we call symbols, words, sentences*

Es ist interessant, die Mannigfaltigkeit der Wort- und Satzarten mit *dem* zu vergleichen, *was* Logiker über den Bau der Sprache gesagt haben.
It is interesting to compare the multiplicity of kinds of word and sentence with what (lit.*with that which*) *logicians have said about the structure of language.*

2 *nichts* with adjectives

(Cf. *Adjectives as Nouns*, p. 61f.)

fest – *solid, fixed*   gegeben – *given*

Diese Mannigfaltigkeit ist *nichts Festes*, ein für allemal *Gegebenes.*
This multiplicity is not something (lit. *nothing*) *fixed, given once and for all.*

3 Preposition *nach*

(Cf. *List of Common Prepositions*, p. 51f.)

Hier gibt es den Sprung *nach vorn* . . .
Here is the leap forward . . .

. . . um *nach Europa* zurückzukehren.
. . . *in order to return* to Europe.

nach einem fünfjährigen Aufenthalt
after *a five-year sojourn*

Die drei Dichtungsarten blühten nicht neben-, sondern *nacheinander.*
The three literary genres flourished not together, but after one another.

Nach Heraklit ist der Krieg der Vater aller Dinge.
According to Heraclitus *war is the father of all things.*

nach Befehlen handeln
obeying orders (lit. *acting* according to orders)

Herstellen eines Gegenstands *nach einer Beschreibung*
Constructing an object from a description

4 Genitive ending *-er*

Es gibt unzählige solch**er** Arten
There are countless kinds (lit.of *such kinds*)

. . . ein Teil ein**er** Tätigkeit, oder ein**er** Lebensform.
. . . *part* of *an activity, or* of *a form of life.*

. . . die Mannigfaltigkeit d**er** Werkzeuge d**er** Sprache und ihr**er** Verwendungsweisen . . .
. . . *the multiplicity* of *the tools in* (lit. of *the) language and* of *the ways they are used* (lit. of *their ways of use*) . . .

Word formation

Complex adjectives derived from nouns
(Cf. *Suffixes in Adjectives,* -ig 2, p. 137f.)

in der *fünfbändig*en Ausgabe
in the five-volume edition

(in fünf Bänden)
(in five volumes)

nach einem *fünfjährig*en Aufenthalt
after a five-year sojourn

(von fünf Jahren)
(of five years)

etwas *Einzigartig*es
something special

(das Einzige seiner Art)
(the only one of its kind)

bei *gleichzeitig*er Verlängerung des Lebensalters
accompanied by an increase in life expectancy

(zur gleichen Zeit)
(at the same time)

eine Gemeinschaft *gleichrangig*er Genossen
a community of comrades of equal status

(gleichen Ranges)
(of equal status)

21

Text

Text: This text is the introduction to a chapter about differences in the psychotherapy of adults and children, and about the historical development of child-psychotherapy. It is taken from a book by the Swiss educator and psychologist *Hans Zulliger* (1893–1965), a pioneer in child psychology.

Quelle: Hans Zulliger, Heilende Kräfte im kindlichen Spiel, 6. Aufl. 1979, Stuttgart, Klett-Cotta.

Task 1:
Translate the heading of the chapter, using the information about the text.

---

1 **Unterschiede zwischen der Erwachsenen- und der Kinderpsychotherapie**
Geschichte der Entwicklung der Kinderpsychotherapie

Wenn wir das Denken der Menschen betrachten, finden wir
5 drei Arten oder Stufen, wobei sich die eine aus der anderen allmählich entwickelt. Die erste, die nach dem vor-magischen Sein der allerersten Lebenszeit in Erscheinung tritt, ist das kindhafte Denken; ich habe versucht, es darzustellen. Es ist dadurch gekennzeichnet, daß es der *primitiven* Wunschwelt
10 entspricht, von ihr dominiert wird, identisch ist mit dem *„Denken des Unbewußten"* und *Symbole* für die Dinge setzt. Schon früh macht sich – neben diesem Denken in Symbolen – die *Realitätsprüfung* bemerkbar und verändert nach und nach das kindliche Denken; das älter werdende Kind lernt die
15 Eigengesetzlichkeit der Umwelt erkennen und begreift den Zusammenhang von Ursache und Wirkung; es beginnt, logisch zu folgern und rationalistisch zu erfassen; noch ist aber sein Denken stark *konkretorisch*, und bei recht vielen Menschen bleibt es auf dieser Stufe stehen. Bei stärker „intellektu-
20 ellen" jungen Leuten tritt während der Zeit der Reifwerdung eine neuerliche Umformung des Denkens ein: sie beginnen *abstraktorisch* zu denken und werden, hauptsächlich in unseren Gymnasien, dazu geschult. Aus der Welt der Erscheinungen und ihrer Wesensgesetze wird das Begriffliche herausde-
25 stilliert und zu neuen Symbolen zusammengefaßt. Das „reine" Denken, das Denken in abstrakten Begriffen, ist eigentlich wiederum ein Symbol-Denken, allerdings auf anderer, höherer Stufe als das Symbol-Denken kleiner Kinder.
30 . . .

Task 2:
Listen and follow the text; then answer the questions.

a Which word is most frequent in the text? Underline it.
b In the first sentence it says that we can identify three stages of thinking. Which three words characterize these three stages? Underline them.
c To which stage does the thinking of small children belong? And to which stage does more „intellectual" thinking belong?

Task 3:
Find the German equivalents in the text and underline them.

a *when we look at human thinking*
b *the first one . . . is childlike thinking*
c *that it . . . is identical with subconscious thinking*
d *parallel with this thinking in symbols*
e *the test of reality . . . alters childhood thinking little by little*
f *his thinking, however, is still strongly concrete*
g *a new transformation of thinking*
h *they begin to think abstractly*
i *pure thinking . . . is symbolic thinking once more*
j *thinking in abstract concepts*
k *the symbolic thinking of small children*

Task 4:
Find the German equivalents in the text and write them down.

a *three varieties or stages*

_____

b *after the pre-magical state of the very first period of life*

_____

c *that it corresponds to the primitive world of wishes*

_____

d *growing older, the child learns to understand the autonomous laws of the environment*

_____

e *with a good many people it remains static at this stage*

_____

f *during the period of maturation* (lit. *ripe-becoming*)

_____

g *from the world of phenomena and its inherent laws*

_____

h *but at another, higher stage*

_____

92

5 Wenn wir das Denken der Menschen betrachten, finden wir drei Arten oder Stufen, wobei sich die eine aus der anderen allmählich entwickelt. Die erste, die nach dem vor-magischen Sein der allerersten Lebenszeit in Erscheinung tritt, ist das kindhafte Denken; ich habe versucht, es darzustellen. Es ist dadurch gekennzeichnet, daß es der *primitiven* Wunschwelt
10 entspricht, von ihr dominiert wird, identisch ist mit dem „*Denken des Unbewußten*" und *Symbole* für die Dinge setzt.

wobei	– here: *among which*	
allmählich	– *gradually*	
in Erscheinung treten	– *to appear, to manifest oneself* (lit. *to step into appearance*)	
versuchen	– _____	
darstellen	– _____	
dadurch	– *by the fact* (lit. *thereby*)	
kennzeichnen	– _____	
(dominiert) von	– (*dominated*) _____	
setzen	– *to set, to put;* here: *to use*	

Task 5:
Check in what context these words occur in the text and supply a suitable English equivalent in each case, either from memory, by guesswork or with the help of the *Basic Word List*.

Task 6:
Read lines 4–11 once again; then answer the questions.

a How are these various stages in thinking related to one another?
b When does *das kindhafte Denken* emerge?
c What is characteristic of this *Denkstufe*?

Schon früh macht sich – neben diesem Denken in Symbolen – die *Realitätsprüfung* bemerkbar und verändert nach und nach das kindliche Denken; das älter werdende Kind lernt die
15 Eigengesetzlichkeit der Umwelt erkennen und begreift den Zusammenhang von Ursache und Wirkung; es beginnt, logisch zu folgern und rationalistisch zu erfassen; noch ist aber sein Denken stark *konkretorisch*, und bei recht vielen Menschen bleibt es auf dieser Stufe stehen.

schon früh	– *very early* (lit. *already early*)
bemerkbar	– *noticeable*
begreifen	– _____

Zusammenhang	– *connection*
Ursache	– _____
Wirkung	– _____
folgern	– *to conclude, to draw conclusions*
erfassen	– *to seize, to comprehend*

Task 7:
Check in what context these words occur in the text and supply a suitable English equivalent in each case, either from memory, by guesswork or with the help of the *Basic Word List*.

Task 8:
Compare the following statements with the text and discuss amongst yourselves to what degree they are compatible with statements made in the text or contradict them.

a Das primitive Denken in Symbolen und die Realitätsprüfung existieren einige Zeit nebeneinander.
b Wenn das Kind älter wird, erkennt es, daß die Welt, in der es lebt, ihre eigenen Gesetze hat.
c Das Kind lernt allmählich auch, wie Ursache und Wirkung zusammenhängen.
d Recht viele Menschen entwickeln das Talent, konkret zu denken.

Bei stärker „intellektuellen" jungen Leuten tritt während der Zeit der Reifwerdung
20 eine neuerliche Umformung des Denkens ein: sie beginnen *abstraktorisch* zu denken und werden, hauptsächlich in unseren Gymnasien, dazu geschult. Aus der Welt der Erscheinungen und ihrer Wesensgesetze wird das Begriffliche herausdestilliert und zu neuen Symbolen zusammengefaßt. Das
25 „reine" Denken, das Denken in abstrakten Begriffen, ist eigentlich wiederum ein Symbol-Denken, allerdings auf anderer, höherer Stufe als das Symbol-Denken kleiner Kinder.

stärker	– *more* (lit. *more strongly*)
Leute	– *people*
eintreten	– *to set in, to occur*
hauptsächlich	– *mainly*
Gymnasium	– *grammar school (secondary school)*
dazu	– *for this purpose, to this end,* here: *to do so* (lit. *thereto*)
schulen	– *to train, to school*
begrifflich	– *conceptual, abstract*
herausdestillieren	– *to distil*
zusammenfassen	– *to combine, to unite*
eigentlich	– *actually*

20 Bei stärker „intellektu-
ellen" jungen Leuten tritt während der Zeit der Reifwerdung
eine neuerliche Umformung des Denkens ein: sie beginnen
abstraktorisch zu denken und werden, hauptsächlich in unseren Gymnasien, dazu geschult. Aus der Welt der Erscheinungen und ihrer Wesensgesetze wird das Begriffliche herausde-
25 stilliert und zu neuen Symbolen zusammengefaßt. Das
„reine" Denken, das Denken in abstrakten Begriffen, ist
eigentlich wiederum ein Symbol-Denken, allerdings auf
anderer, höherer Stufe als das Symbol-Denken kleiner
Kinder.

Task 9:
Read lines 19–29 once again; then answer the questions.

a In what group of persons does abstract thinking develop?
b By what means can this development be encouraged?
c How do abstract concepts arise?
d In how far does the third stage in thinking resemble the first and what is the difference?

Task 10:
Read the whole text (p. 92) through once again and summarize it in your own words.

Task 11:
Discuss amongst yourselves what connection there might be between these stages in thinking and psychotherapy. (Think of the title of the book and the title of the chapter.)

Word formation

1 Basic word *scheiden*

scheiden, schied, geschieden – *to separate, to divide*

Derivatives:

unzählige *verschiedene* Arten der Verwendung
countless different *kinds of use*

Man spricht von *verschiedenen* Modalitäten.
We speak of various modes (of communication).

Der Verstand *unterscheidet* zwischen möglich und unmöglich.
The intellect distinguishes between possible and impossible.

Unterschiede zwischen der Erwachsenen- und der Kinderpsychotherapie
Differences *in the Psychotherapy of Adults and Children*

jeder Rang*unterschied* zwischen Menschen
every difference *in status between human beings*

2 Prefix *aller-*
(Cf. *Prefixes*, p. 124)

der erste | der allererste
the first | *the very first*

3 Prefix *heraus-*
(Cf. *Prefixes*, p. 128)

destilieren | herausdestillieren
to distil | *to distil, to condense*

geben | herausgeben
to give | *to edit*

4 Prefix *um-*
This prefix has two different meanings (cf. *Prefixes*, p. 131).

geben | umgeben
to give | *to surround*

fassen | umfassen
to seize, to grasp | *to comprise, to contain*

die Welt | die Umwelt
the world | *the environment*

formen | umformen
to form | *to transform*

5 Prefix *zusammen-*
(Cf. *Prefixes*, p. 134)

fassen | zusammenfassen
to seize, to grasp | *to combine, to summarize*

wirken | zusammenwirken
to work, to have an effect | *to work together, to have a combined effect*

hängen | zusammenhängen (mit)
to hang | *to be joined (with), to be connected (with), to be related (to)*

schauen | zusammenschauend
to look, to view | *viewing everything as a whole*

6 Suffix *-bar*

(Cf. *Suffixes in Adjectives*, p. 136)

| bemerken | bemerkbar |
| *to notice* | *noticeable* |

| realisieren | realisierbar |
| *to realize* | *realizable* |

Note:
Instead of the usual adjectives *abstrakt* and *konkret Zulliger* employs the unusual forms *abstraktorisch* and *konkretorisch* (which cannot be found in the dictionary) in the sense of "having a tendency towards the abstract or the concrete".

7 Suffix *-haft*

(Cf. *Suffixes in Adjectives*, p. 137)

| Kind | kindhaft |
| *child* | *childlike, childish* |

22

Text

Text: In his book on the social psychology of prejudices the author speaks of the prejudices which the strata of a society exhibit towards one another. Then he deals with the conflict between the generations. One of the forms taken by this "Chauvinism of Age-Groups" is the suppression of young people. The text is from this section.

Quelle: Manfred Koch-Hillebrecht, Der Stoff, aus dem die Dummheit ist, Verlag C. H. Beck, München 1978, S. 184.

4.4.1. Unterdrückung der Jugend

Vor der Jugend haben die meisten Kulturen eine verborgene Angst. Der Psychoanalytiker Bernfeld (1931) meint, daß Erziehung nicht ohne die „männliche Urreaktion" gegenüber dem Kind zustandekomme, die Tötungstendenz. Erziehung
5 sei eine in vielen Formen sublimierte Todesdrohung. In den jungen Menschen lauert die Gefahr, die eigene Kultur zu zerstören. Die Angst vor dem destruktiven Potential der Jugend hat der amerikanische Soziologe Talcott Parsons
10 besonders gut beschrieben, wenn er meint, in jeder neuen Generation werde die Kultur von einer Horde Wilder bedroht. Die Sozialisation, der Versuch, die jungen Leute nicht nur mit der herrschenden Kultur vertraut zu machen, sondern den Heranwachsenden diese Kultur als die ihre
15 einzuverleiben, sei ein Grundprozeß jeder Erziehung.
. . .

Task 1:
Listen and follow the text. Translate the first sentence *(verborgen – hidden; Angst vor – fear of)*, then answer the questions.

a Which two authorities are mentioned?
b What shows that the author is quoting the *Meinungen (opinions)* of these experts?
c Which other expressions are used synonymously with *Jugend*? Put a circle round them.
d Which two expressions do you recognize as being negative views of young people?

Task 2:
Find the German equivalents in the text and underline them.

a *the tendency to kill*
b *a sublimated threat of death*
c *threatened by a horde of savages*
d *a basic procedure in every education process*

Task 3:
Find the German equivalents in the text and write them down.

a *. . . lurks the danger of the destruction of* (lit. *to destroy*) *their own culture*

_____

_____

b *Fear of the . . . has been especially well described by Parsons* (lit. *Parsons has described the fear*)

_____

_____

c *. . . to familiarize the young people* (lit. *make the young people familiar*) *with the dominant culture*

_____

_____

Task 4:
Look up the prefixes *Unter-* and *Ur-* (cf. *Prefixes*, p. 132) and decide what the English equivalents to *Unterdrückung* and *Urreaktion* are.

drücken	– *to press*
Unterdrückung	– _____
ohne	– *without*
männlich	– *male, masculine*
Urreaktion	– _____

gegenüber	– *to, with regard to*
zustandekommen	– *to come about, to take place*
heranwachsen(d)	– *grow(ing) up*
der/die/das ihre	– *theirs, their own*
einverleiben	– *to assimilate, to take in*

Task 5:
Read the text once again and answer the questions.

a Which three further passages in the text express more or less the same as the first sentence? Underline them.
b Which statements represent the author's opinion?
c What is *Bernfeld*'s view of education?
d What is *Parson*'s opinion?
e How is *Sozialisation* defined in the text?

Text: This text is also from the book on the social psychology of prejudices and the significance of stereotypes. In the passages preceding the text the author says that stereotypes are always based on a few marked features of reality. The more removed things or people are from us (in time or space) the less we know about them.

Quelle: Manfred Koch-Hillebrecht, Der Stoff, aus dem die Dummheit ist, Verlag H. C. Beck, München 1978, S. 109.

1	**Gesetz der Distanz**

. . . Auch in der Völkerpsychologie gibt es ein Gesetz der Distanz. Je weiter ein Volk entfernt ist, um so geringer und um so einförmiger sind unsere Kenntnisse von ihm. Auch läßt
5 uns unsere Unterscheidungsfähigkeit bei sehr fremden Völkern im Stich. Wir können allenfalls zwischen einem Nordfranzosen und einem Provençalen unterscheiden, zwischen einem Milanesen und einem Sizilianer, aber Nord- und Südjapaner oder Nordthailänder und Südthailänder unterscheiden
10 wir nicht mehr. Wir wissen, daß die Mädchen von Valencia als temperamentvoll gelten, jedoch daß die Mädchen von Chiengmai (im Norden Thailands) besonders schön sein sollen, ist uns unbekannt. Wir können den Unterschied zwischen einem Koreaner und einem Japaner schwerlich feststellen.
15 Dieser Unterschied (die Koreaner gelten als etwas gröber und stärker) ist jedoch für jeden Japaner auffällig. Der Japaner hingegen kann auf der Straße Deutsche nicht von Amerikanern oder von anderen Europäern unterscheiden. . . .

Task 1:
Listen and follow the text; then read it again to yourself and answer the questions.

a   What terms are used for peoples or groups of people in the text? Put a circle round each of them.
b   Who does the author mean when he says *wir, uns* and *unser?*
c   What sort of law is mentioned in the first sentence?
d   Which groups of people can Germans distinguish between and which not?
e   In the middle of the text girls from two different places are mentioned. Where are the places? What is the German equivalent of *girl(s)?*
f   What examples can you find in the text of the fact that Asiatics all look similar to Europeans and vice versa?

. . . Auch in der Völkerpsychologie gibt es ein Gesetz der Distanz. Je weiter ein Volk entfernt ist, um so geringer und um so einförmiger sind unsere Kenntnisse von ihm. Auch läßt
5 uns unsere Unterscheidungsfähigkeit bei sehr fremden Völkern im Stich.

je . . . um so . . .	– the . . . the . . .
Kenntnis, -se	– knowledge
Fähigkeit	– ability
im Stich lassen	– to abandon, to leave in the lurch

Task 2:
Decide according to context (lines 2–6) to which English word each of these six German words corresponds: *weiter – entfernt – geringer – einförmiger – sehr – fremd.*

alien, unfamiliar   – _____

distant, remote   – _____

further, farther   – _____

more uniform   – _____

smaller, poorer   – _____

very   – _____

Task 3:
Find the German equivalents in the text and underline them.

a   *that the girls of . . . are considered to be lively*
b   *that the girls of . . . are said to be especially beautiful*
c   *the Koreans are considered to be more crudely and strongly built*
d   *on the other hand the Japanese cannot distinguish . . .*
e   *on the street*

Task 4:
Find the German equivalents in the text and write them down.

a   *At most we can distinguish between . . .*

_____

b   *we do not distinguish any longer*

_____

c   *We can hardly detect the difference . . .*

_____

d   *This difference is, however, evident to every Japanese.*

_____

e   *We know that . . .*

_____

f   *we do not know that . . .* (lit. *that . . . is unknown to us*)

Task 5:
Reproduce in your own words the *Gesetz der Distanz in der Völkerpsychologie* and illustrate it by means of examples from the text.

97

Grammar

1 Subjunctive I – Reported speech

The forms *komme, sei, werde* are subjunctive forms of *kommt, ist wird*. These forms emphasize the fact that the author is quoting the statements or opinions of others (cf. *Subjunctive: Forms*, p. 95, and *Reported Speech*, p. 97).

Bernfeld meint, daß Erziehung nicht ohne die „männliche Urre-aktion" gegenüber dem Kind zustande*komme,* die Tötungsten-denz. Erziehung *sei* eine sublimierte Todesdrohung.
Bernfeld is of the opionion that education cannot take place without the "primeval masculine reaction" to the child, the ten-dency to kill. Education is a sublimated threat of death.

. . . *er* (Parsons) *meint,* in jeder neuen Generation *werde* die Kultur von einer Horde Wilder bedroht. Die Sozialisation . . . *sei* ein Grundprozeß jeder Erziehung.
. . . *he (Parsons) expresses the opinion that with every new gener-ation culture is threatened by a horde of savages. Socialization . . . is a basic procedure in every education process.*

2 Verbs *gelten als* and *sollen*

These verbs emphasize the fact that the author is reporting what he knows from hearsay:

Wir wissen, daß die Mädchen von Valencia *als* temperamentvoll *gelten,* jedoch daß die Mädchen von Chiengmai besonders schön sein *sollen,* ist uns unbekannt.
We know that the girls of Valencia are considered to be lively, but we do not know that the girls of Chiengmai are said to be especially beautiful.

3 *je . . . um so* in comparisons

The conjunction *je* introduces a dependent clause which is followed by *um so* (or *desto*). *Je . . . um so/desto* are always accompanied by adjectives/adverbs in the comparative form. (cf. *Adjectives: Comparison*, p. 60).

Je weiter ein Volk entfernt ist, *um so geringer und um so einförmi-ger* sind unsere Kenntnisse von ihm.
The more remote a nation is, the poorer and (the) more uniform *is our knowledge of it.*

Word formation

1 Suffix *-fähig*
(Cf. *Suffixes in Adjectives*, p. 137)

Unterscheidung	unterscheidungs*fähig*
distinction, difference	*able to make distinctions*

2 Suffix *-er*
(Cf. *Suffixes in Nouns, -er 2*, p. 142)

Korea, Sizilien, Europa	Korea*ner,* Sizilia*ner,* Euro-pä*er*
Korea, Sicily, Europe	*Korean(s), Sicilian(s), Euro-pean(s)*

3 Prefix *zer-*
(Cf. *Prefixes*, p. 135)

stören – *to disturb*	*zer*stören – *to destroy*

4 Prefix *heran-*
(Cf. *Prefixes*, p. 128)

wachsen – *to grow*	*heran*wachsen – *to grow up*

5 Basic word *kennen*

kennen, kannte, gekannt – *to know*

der *bekannte* Historiker
the well-known *historian*

in nie *gekannt*em Maße
*on a previously un*known *scale*

Das Kind lernt die Eigengesetzlichkeit . . . *erkennen*
The child learns to understand (lit. *recognize) the autonomous laws* . . .

. . . *um so* einförmiger sind unsere *Kenntnisse*
. . . *the more uniform is our* knowledge

Das *ist* uns un*bekannt*
We do not know *that*

Das kindhafte Denken ist dadurch *gekennzeichnet,* daß . . .
Infantile thinking is characterized *by the fact that* . . .

Text

Text: The German Federal Government commissioned the psychologist *Koch-Hillebrecht* to investigate how other people see the Germans. In the first three chapters of his book *Das Deutschenbild (The German Image Abroad)* he deals with the way individual peoples see the Germans, the way groups of peoples see the Germans and typical images of the Germans which may be encountered throughout the world. Parts of the fourth chapter *Bilder bei soziographischen Gruppen* are reproduced in this reader, in this and the following chapters.

Quelle: Manfred Koch-Hillebrecht, Das Deutschenbild, Verlag C. H. Beck, München 1977, Beck'sche Schwarze Reihe, Bd. 162, S. 146–153.

4. Bilder bei soziographischen Gruppen

Der Nationalstaat ist ein starkes Band, das die Menschen umfaßt und beeinflußt. Insofern ist die Färbung des Deutschenbildes in hohem Grade davon abhängig, welcher Nation
5 jemand angehört. Insofern war es auch sinnvoll, vom Deutschenbild bei einzelnen Völkern und bei Völkergruppen zu sprechen.
Es muß aber betont werden, daß die Rede vom Deutschenbild eines Volkes eine Simplifizierung bedeutet. Die Deut-
10 schenbilder innerhalb der Völker sind nämlich durchaus nicht einförmig. Das Nationale ist ein wichtiger Faktor der Stereotypenbildung, aber bestimmt nicht der einzige: es waren uns schon die religionssoziologischen Einflüsse aufgefallen (beim puritanischen Image), weltanschauliche bei den kommunisti-
15 schen Ländern und schließlich rein materielle in den Entwicklungsländern. Die groben Züge des Deutschenbildes werden oft vom Nationalen her geprägt, die feineren oft von anderen Gruppenbindungen.
Es gibt nun Gruppen mit ausgesprochenem Gruppenbe-
20 wußtsein, in denen das Verbundenheitsgefühl mit der Gruppe die nationalen Gefühle überdecken kann. Dann entstehen internationale gruppenspezifische Deutschenbilder. Diese sollen jetzt besprochen werden.
Drei soziographische Gruppen tendieren in vielen Ländern
25 der Welt dazu, eher etwas deutschfeindlich zu sein, die Intelligenz, die feinen Leute und die Frauen. Eine andere international verbreitete einflußreiche Gruppe verhehlt nicht deutliche deutschfreundliche Neigungen: die Militärs.

Task 1
Listen and follow the text; then read it to yourself and answer the questions.

a Which factor which influences the German image abroad is mentioned in the first section of the text (lines 2–7)? Underline the relevant word.
b How many factors are mentioned in the second section of the text (lines 8–18)? Underline the relevant words.
c Which images of the Germans are mentioned in the third section (lines 19–23)? Underline the relevant expression.
d How many groups are mentioned in the fourth section (lines 24–28)? Underline them.
e Which of these groups might one most readily describe as being amicably disposed towards Germans? Underline the equivalent of "pro-German" in the text.

Der Nationalstaat ist ein starkes Band, das die Menschen umfaßt und beeinflußt. Insofern ist die Färbung des Deutschenbildes in hohem Grade davon abhängig, welcher Nation jemand angehört. Insofern war es auch sinnvoll, vom Deutschenbild bei einzelnen Völkern und bei Völkergruppen zu sprechen.

der Staat	–
stark	–
das Band	– *bond, tie*
umfassen	– *to clasp, to embrace, to encompass*
insofern	– *thus far, in this respect, in so far*
die Färbung	– *colouring*
der Grad	–
abhängig von	–
jemand	– *someone*
angehören	–
sinnvoll	–

Task 2:
Check in what context these words appear in lines 2–7 of the text and supply a suitable English equivalent in each case, either from memory, by guesswork or with the help of the *Basic Word List*.

Task 3:
Read lines 2–7 once again; then answer the questions.

a What does the text say about the nation-state?
b What strongly influences the German image abroad?
c Which stereotypes has the author apparently talked about earlier?

10 Es muß aber betont werden, daß die Rede vom Deutschenbild eines Volkes eine Simplifizierung bedeutet. Die Deutschenbilder innerhalb der Völker sind nämlich durchaus nicht
einförmig. Das Nationale ist ein wichtiger Faktor der Stereotypenbildung, aber bestimmt nicht der einzige: es waren uns
15 schon die religionssoziologischen Einflüsse aufgefallen (beim
puritanischen Image), weltanschauliche bei den kommunistischen Ländern und schließlich rein materielle in den Entwicklungsländern. Die groben Züge des Deutschenbildes werden
oft vom Nationalen her geprägt, die feineren oft von anderen
Gruppenbindungen.

Task 4:
Underline all those words (in lines 8–18 of the text) whose
meaning is apparent. Put a circle round the two negatives.

Task 5:
Find the German equivalents in the text and underline them.

a   *it must be emphasized*
b   *by no means uniform*
c   *an important factor in the forming of stereotypes*
d   *certainly not the only one*
e   *we had already noticed*
f   *ideological influences*
g   *in the developing countries*
h   *the broad outlines are shaped*
i   *by other group ties*

Task 6:
Read lines 8–18 once again; then answer the questions.

a   Why is it a simplification to talk about the German image with
    particular peoples?
b   What influences play a role in the formation of stereotypes?
c   What factor is characteristic of the German image in devel-
    oping countries?
d   What factors lead to more complex images of the Germans?

20 Es gibt nun Gruppen mit ausgesprochenem Gruppenbewußtsein, in denen das Verbundenheitsgefühl mit der Gruppe
die nationalen Gefühle überdecken kann. Dann entstehen
internationale gruppenspezifische Deutschenbilder. Diese
sollen jetzt besprochen werden.

das Gefühl, -e	– *feeling*
überdecken	– *to overlay, to eclipse*
entstehen	– *to arise, to emerge, to result*
besprechen	– *to discuss*

Task 7:
Find the German equivalents (in lines 19–23 of the text) and
underline them.

a   *a pronounced group consciousness*
b   *the sense of a common bond*

Task 8:
Read lines 19–23 once again; then answer the questions.

a   What is often stronger than national sentiments?
b   What is the consequence of this?
c   What intention is declared by the author in lines 22–23?

25 Drei soziographische Gruppen tendieren in vielen Ländern
der Welt dazu, eher etwas deutschfeindlich zu sein, die Intelligenz, die feinen Leute und die Frauen. Eine andere international verbreitete einflußreiche Gruppe verhehlt nicht deutliche deutschfreundliche Neigungen: die Militärs.

eher	– *sooner, more, rather*
etwas	– *somewhat, a little*
die Frau, -en	– _____
verbreitet	– *widespread, common*
verhehlen	– *to conceal*
deutlich	– _____
freundlich	– *friendly*
die Neigung, -en	– _____

Task 9:
Check in what context these words appear in the text (lines
24–28) and supply a suitable English equivalent in each case,
either from memory, by guesswork or with the help of the *Basic
Word List.*

Task 10:
Put a circle round the negative in the last part of the text.
Underline the two anonyms. Then answer the questions.

a   Which groups tend to be hostile towards Germans?
b   What does the text say about the military? Translate this
    sentence, lines 26–28.

4. Bilder bei soziographischen Gruppen

Der Nationalstaat ist ein starkes Band, das die Menschen umfaßt und beeinflußt. Insofern ist die Färbung des Deutschenbildes in hohem Grade davon abhängig, welcher Nation jemand angehört. Insofern war es auch sinnvoll, vom Deutschenbild bei einzelnen Völkern und bei Völkergruppen zu sprechen.

Es muß aber betont werden, daß die Rede vom Deutschenbild eines Volkes eine Simplifizierung bedeutet. Die Deutschenbilder innerhalb der Völker sind nämlich durchaus nicht einförmig. Das Nationale ist ein wichtiger Faktor der Stereotypenbildung, aber bestimmt nicht der einzige: es waren uns schon die religionssoziologischen Einflüsse aufgefallen (beim puritanischen Image), weltanschauliche bei den kommunistischen Ländern und schließlich rein materielle in den Entwicklungsländern. Die groben Züge des Deutschenbildes werden oft vom Nationalen her geprägt, die feineren oft von anderen Gruppenbindungen.

Es gibt nun Gruppen mit ausgesprochenem Gruppenbewußtsein, in denen das Verbundenheitsgefühl mit der Gruppe die nationalen Gefühle überdecken kann. Dann entstehen internationale gruppenspezifische Deutschenbilder. Diese sollen jetzt besprochen werden.

Drei soziographische Gruppen tendieren in vielen Ländern der Welt dazu, eher etwas deutschfeindlich zu sein, die Intelligenz, die feinen Leute und die Frauen. Eine andere international verbreitete einflußreiche Gruppe verhehlt nicht deutliche deutschfreundliche Neigungen: die Militärs.

Task 11:
Read the whole text once again; then complete the summary given below by quoting from the text.

1 Es gibt verschiedene Faktoren, die das _____ _____ beeinflussen.

2 Das Deutschenbild eines Menschen ist davon _____, welche Nationalität er hat.

3 Es gibt auch andere _____: religionssoziologische, _____ und materialistische.

4 Das Gefühl, einer bestimmten Gruppe anzugehören, ist oft stärker als _____.

5 Das Ergebnis sind _____ Deutschenbilder.

6 Die Intellektuellen, die Oberschicht und die Frauen sind _____.

7 Die Militärs vieler Länder haben _____ Tendenzen.

Grammar

1 Verb *auffallen*

jemandem fällt etwas auf (The subject is *etwas*.)
something strikes somebody/somebody notices something

Was fällt uns an den Stereotypen auf?
What strikes us/What do we notice about the stereotypes?

. . . waren uns schon die religionssoziologischen Einflüsse aufgefallen . . .
. . . we had already noticed the religious-sociological influences . . .

2 *es* used as a filler

Es occurs sometimes as a filler in initial position in independent clauses. There is no direct equivalent in English (cf. *Word Order (Subject), „es"*, p. 110f.).

Es waren uns schon die religionssoziologischen Einflüsse aufgefallen . . .
We had already noticed the religious-sociological influences . . .

3 One form – two genders – two meanings

der Militär, -s – *army officer, military man*
das Militär (no plural) – *military, armed forces*

Eine andere Gruppe verhehlt nicht deutliche deutschfreundliche Neigungen: die Militärs.
Another group does not conceal its distinct pro-German inclinations: the military men.

der Band, ⸚e – *volume (of a book)*
das Band, ⸚er – *ribbon, tape, band, bond*

Der Nationalstaat ist ein starkes Band, das die Menschen umfaßt und beeinflußt.
The nation-state is a strong bond which embraces and influences people.

Der Historiker *Lothar Gall* stellt jedem Band einen einführenden Essay voran.
The historian Lothar Gall introduces each volume with an introductory essay.

Word formation

1 Basic word *binden*

binden, band, gebunden – *to bind, to tie*

Derivatives:
das Band – *ribbon, tape, band, bond*
der Band – *volume (of a book)*

die Gruppenbindung – *group tie*
das Verbundenheitsgefühl – *sense of a common bond*

2 Basic word *wissen*

wissen, wußte, gewußt – *to know*

Derivatives:
die Wissenschaft – *science*
das nötige Wissen – *the necessary knowledge*

das Gruppenbewußtsein – *group consciousness*
das Unbewußte – *unconsciousness*

3 Suffix *-förmig*

(Cf. *Suffixes in Adjectives,* p. 137)

Die Deutschenbilder sind durchaus nicht einförmig.
The German images are by no means uniform.

4 Prefix *be-*

(Cf. *Prefixes,* pp. 125–126).

beeinflussen – *to influence*   (Einfluß – *influence*)
sich beteiligen – *to participate*   (Teil – *part*)
beschleunigen – *to accelerate*   (schleunig – *quick, prompt*)
begreifen – *to comprehend*   (greifen – *to grasp, to seize*)
besprechen – *to discuss*   (sprechen – *to speak*)
beschreiben – *to describe*   (schreiben – *to write*)

5 Prefix *ab-*

(Cf. *Prefixes,* p. 124).

abhängig von – *dependent on*   (hängen – *to hang*)
Abwanderung – *moving away, migration* (wandern – *to wander*)
abreißen – *to tear off, to break off*   (reißen – *to tear*)
absehen von – *to disregard*   (sehen – *to see*)

Text

Text und Quelle: s. Kapitel 23.

---

4. Bilder bei soziographischen Gruppen

4.1. Intelligenz

Die Intelligenz ist, von wenigen Ländern abgesehen, nicht deutschfreundlich. Der Grund hierfür liegt vor allem im reaktionären, militaristischen Image der Deutschen. Deutschland gilt hier fast als ein Fortschrittsfeind. Frankreich hat es viel besser verstanden, ein progressives Image zu projizieren, das auf die Intellektuellen der ganzen Welt als Vorbild wirkt.

Frankreich mit seiner revolutionären Tradition, seinem Nationalfeiertag, der den Sturm auf die Bastille feiert, England mit seinen demokratischen Idealen und erst recht Rußland mit seiner marxistischen Ideologie und neuerdings Kuba und China sind die Vorbilder dieser Kreise. Manchmal ist auch ein unmittelbarer Einfluß kommunistischer Propaganda zu spüren. Eins kommt hier zum anderen. Deutschland tendiert dazu, seine großen Geister aus dem konservativen Lager mehr zu ehren und zu schätzen als seine revolutionären Söhne. Uns geht es leichter über die Lippen, von „unserem Hegel", „unserem Bismarck" zu reden als von „unserem Marx". Auch unsere Straßen werden eher nach Bismarck als nach Marx benannt.

Nicht nur die jungen Wissenschaftler stehen oft links, sondern auch vor allem die jungen Künstler. Hier handelt es sich um ein so verbreitetes und leicht erklärbares Phänomen, daß man kaum Theorien wie die von Mannheims freischwebenden intellektuellen Gruppen zuhilfe nehmen muß, um eine Erklärung zu finden. Frankreich hat es in seiner Kunstpropaganda in aller Welt sehr viel besser verstanden, ein progressives Bild von sich zu geben. In Japan ist moderne Kunst gleichbedeutend mit französischer Kunst.

In vielen Ländern sind die deutschen Beiträge zur abstrakten Kunst erst sehr viel später und mit großer Überraschung wahrgenommen worden. Man traute den Deutschen den Blauen Reiter und den Expressionismus ebenso wenig zu wie Leistungen auf dem Gebiet der elektronischen Musik.

Auch hier fehlt uns Deutschen oft die glückliche Hand im Umgang mit unseren eigenen Intelligenzgruppen: so müssen wir es mit ansehen, daß die Eierköpfe vieler Länder, die Studenten, die Professoren, die abstrakten Maler, die Literaten und Photographen – und auch die Journalisten eher deutschfeindlich sind.

Georg Wilhelm Friedrich Hegel (1770–1831), deutscher Philosoph
Otto von Bismarck (1815–1898), deutscher Staatsmann
Karl Marx (1818–1883), deutscher revolutionärer Schriftsteller, schrieb *Das Kapital*, eine Kritik des kapitalistischen Systems.
Karl Mannheim (1893–1947), deutscher Soziologe
„Der Blaue Reiter", eine Gruppe von expressionistischen Malern (*painters*), 1911 in München gegründet.

Task 1:
Discuss among yourselves what you understand by *die Intelligenz* as a sociographic group.

Task 2:
Read the text to yourself and underline all proper names (of persons, countries, etc.).

Task 3:
Listen and follow the text. Then find the main points in each of the five paragraphs of the text. Compare your results.

Lines

3 – 9: _____

10 – 22: _____

23 – 31: _____

32 – 36: _____

37 – 42: _____

Task 4:
Find the German equivalents in the text and write them down.

a . . . *which serves as an example to the intellectuals*

_____

b . . . *are the examples to these circles*

_____

c . . . *has known how to project a progressive image*

_____

d . . . *has known how to give a progressive image of herself*

Die Intelligenz ist, von wenigen Ländern abgesehen, nicht deutschfreundlich. Der Grund hierfür liegt vor allem im reaktionären, militaristischen Image der Deutschen. Deutschland gilt hier fast als ein Fortschrittsfeind. Frankreich hat es viel besser verstanden, ein progressives Image zu projizieren, das auf die Intellektuellen der ganzen Welt als Vorbild wirkt.

---

abgesehen von	– *apart from, except for*
hierfür	– *for this*
fast	– *almost*
der Fortschritt	– *progress*

Task 5:
Read lines 3–8 once again; then answer the questions.

a What is the attitude of *die Intelligenz*?
b What is the reason for this attitude?
c What does the text have to say about France?

> 10 Frankreich mit seiner revolutionären Tradition, seinem Nationalfeiertag, der den Sturm auf die Bastille feiert, England mit seinen demokratischen Idealen und erst recht Rußland mit seiner marxistischen Ideologie und neuerdings Kuba und China sind die Vorbilder dieser Kreise. Manchmal ist
> 15 auch ein unmittelbarer Einfluß kommunistischer Propaganda zu spüren. Eins kommt hier zum anderen. Deutschland tendiert dazu, seine großen Geister aus dem konservativen Lager mehr zu ehren und zu schätzen als seine revolutionären Söhne. Uns geht es leichter über die Lippen, von „unserem
> 20 Hegel","unserem Bismarck" zu reden als von „unserem Marx". Auch unsere Straßen werden eher nach Bismarck als nach Marx benannt.

der Feiertag	– holiday
feiern	– to celebrate
erst recht	– all the more, particularly
neuerdings	– recently
das Lager	– camp
leicht	– easy
reden von	– to talk of

Task 6:
Find the German equivalents in the text and write them down.

a *sometimes a direct influence can be noticed*

_____

b *to honour and to value her great minds more . . .*

_____

c *our streets are more likely to be named . . .*

Task 7:
Check in what context the following expressions occur in the text and explain them.

a Eins kommt hier zum anderen.
b Uns geht es leichter über die Lippen, . . .
c . . . die Vorbilder dieser Kreise.

> Nicht nur die jungen Wissenschaftler stehen oft links, sondern auch vor allem die jungen Künstler. Hier handelt es sich um
> 25 ein so verbreitetes und leicht erklärbares Phänomen, daß man kaum Theorien wie die von Mannheims freischwebenden intellektuellen Gruppen zuhilfe nehmen muß, um eine Erklärung zu finden. Frankreich hat es in seiner Kunstpropaganda in aller Welt sehr viel besser verstanden, ein progressives Bild
> 30 von sich zu geben. In Japan ist moderne Kunst gleichbedeutend mit französischer Kunst.

links	– _____
die Kunst	– _____

verbreitet	– _____
erklären	– _____
kaum	– _____
freischwebend	– *free-floating, independent*
zuhilfe nehmen	– *to use, to bring into play*
bedeuten	– *to mean*
hier handelt es sich um	– *this is*

Task 8:
Check in what context these words appear in the text and supply a suitable English equivalent in each case, either from memory, by guesswork or with the help of the *Basic Word List*.

Task 9:
Read lines 23–31 once again; then answer the questions.

a What phenomenon is so easy to explain?
b What term do sociologists use for this phenomenon?
c What does the author have to say here about the theories of sociologists?
d What does the author have to say about French propaganda and about its effects?

> In vielen Ländern sind die deutschen Beiträge zur abstrakten Kunst erst sehr viel später und mit großer Überraschung wahrgenommen worden. Man traute den Deutschen den Blauen Reiter und den Expressionismus ebenso wenig zu wie
> 35 Leistungen auf dem Gebiet der elektronischen Musik.

der Beitrag	– *contribution*
die Überraschung	– *surprise*
jemandem etwas zutrauen	– *to credit somebody with something*

Task 10:
Find the German equivalents in the text and write them down.

a *. . . were not noticed until very much later*

_____

b *just as little as achievements in the field of music*

_____

Task 11:
Read lines 32–36 once again; then answer the questions.

a What was a surprise in many countries?
b Why were people so surprised?

40 | Auch hier fehlt uns Deutschen oft die glückliche Hand im Umgang mit unseren eigenen Intelligenzgruppen: so müssen wir es mit ansehen, daß die Eierköpfe vieler Länder, die Studenten, die Professoren, die abstrakten Maler, die Literaten und Photographen – und auch die Journalisten eher deutschfeindlich sind.

(etwas) fehlt uns	– we lack (something)
glücklich	– lucky
im Umgang mit	– in dealing with
mit ansehen	– to stand by and watch
der Eierkopf, ̈e	– egghead

Task 12:
Read lines 37–42 once again; then answer the questions.

a What is the position of German *Intelligenzgruppen* in their own country?
b What is the outcome of this position?
c What expressions indicate the author's regret about this?
d What sort of people is meant by the term *die Literaten* in this context?

Task 13:
Read the whole text once again and answer the questions.

a What representatives of *die Intelligenz* are named by the author?
b What leanings does he generally ascribe to the intellectuals?
c What image does *die Intelligenz* have of each of the countries mentioned in the text?

Grammar

1 Pronouns *der, die, das* and *eine, einer, eines*

Theorien wie *die* von Mannheims freischwebenden Intelligenzgruppen . . .
Theories *such as* that *of Mannheim's free-floating intellectual groups* . . .

In Amerika lebt *sein Name* als *der* eines Begründers ihrer Kenntnis von sich selbst.
In America his name *lives on as* that *of a founder of their knowledge of themselves.*

. . . die Müller-Lyersche Täuschung, die als *eines* der klassischen *Beispiele* optischer Täuschung gelten kann.
. . . *the Müller-Lyer illusion which can be regarded as* one *of the classic* examples *of optical illusions.*

Die Linien sind gleich lang, obwohl *die eine* wesentlich länger erscheint.
Both lines *are equally long although* one *appears to be considerably longer.*

. . . der Versuch, den Heranwachsenden *diese Kultur* als *die ihre* einzuverleiben.
. . . *the attempt to implant* this culture *within the adolescents as* their own.

2 Verb *fehlen*

etwas fehlt – *something is lacking*
jemandem fehlt etwas (The subject is *etwas*.) – *somebody lacks something*

Uns Deutschen fehlt die glückliche Hand im Umgang mit unseren eigenen Intellektuellen.
We Germans lack the lucky touch in dealing with our own intellectuals.

3 Verbal expression *es handelt sich um*

handeln – *to act, to behave*
es handelt sich um (etwas) – *it is about, it concerns (something)*

hier handelt es sich um – *this is, here we are dealing with*
Hier handelt es sich um ein so verbreitetes Phänomen . . .
This is such a widespread phenomenon . . .

Word formation

1 Basic word *Grund*

Der Grund hierfür liegt im reaktionären, militaristischen Image der Deutschen.
The reason for this lies in the reactionary, militaristic image of the Germans.

. . . haben wir Grund zum Mißtrauen.
. . . we have grounds for mistrust.

Grundfragen der Philosophie
Fundamental Questions of Philosophy

Die Sozialisation ist ein Grundprozeß jeder Erziehung.
Socialization is a basic procedure in every education process.

Das Buch gründet sich auf eingehende Studien . . .
The book is based on thorough studies . . .

Von Humboldt gilt als Begründer der Klimalehre . . .
Von Humboldt is considered to be the founder of the theory of climate . . .

„Der Blaue Reiter", 1911 in München gegründet.
"Der Blaue Reiter", founded in Munich in 1911.

2 Complex adjectives derived from verbs

weitverbreitet – *widespread*   (verbreiten – *to spread*)
weitgehend – *far-reaching, extensive*   (gehen – *to go*)
gleichbedeutend – *synonymous*   (bedeuten – *to mean*)
freischwebend – *free-floating*   (schweben – *to float*)
sogenannt – *so-called*   (nennen – *to name, to call*)

Text

Text und Quelle: s. Kapitel 23.

4. Bilder bei soziographischen Gruppen
4.4. Militärs

Eine große Gruppe oft nicht gerade wenig einflußreicher Herren tendiert dagegen dazu, deutschfreundlich zu reagieren: Die Militärs der ganzen Welt. Sowohl ein Feldwebel der amerikanischen Marine, wie ein Offizier indischer Gurkha-Truppen, wie der Anführer einer südamerikanischen Militärjunta wird vermutlich einen gewissen Hang zur Deutschenfreundlichkeit haben. Ein Erlebnis aus Nepal mag die Gründe für die Deutschenfreundlichkeit der Militärs demonstrieren. Der Militärattaché an der indischen Botschaft in Kathmandu gehörte einem Gurkha-Regiment an. Er ist sehr erfreut, einen Deutschen zu sehen. Er büffelt gerade, um eine Prüfung zu bestehen, die er braucht, um in den indischen Generalstab aufgenommen zu werden. Hierzu liest er die Schriften deutscher Militärtheoretiker, teilweise im Originaltext. Im Augenblick studiert er die Schlachten Rommels in Nordafrika. Er lädt mich am nächsten Tag zum Tee ein und holt ein Buch hervor, das er wie eine Bibel heilig hält. Es ist Clausewitzens Schrift „Vom Kriege" in einer billigen Volksausgabe. Er reicht mir den Band und ich muß ihm die deutschen Sätze langsam vorsprechen, so wie bei einer Dichterlesung. Verzückt sitzt der junge indische Offizier und hört, wie ich ihm die deutschen Sätze langsam vorlese, als seien es Gedichte von Hölderlin.
Ein Offizier, der sich Clausewitz wie ein Gedicht vortragen läßt, kann kein Feind der Deutschen sein. Auch bei Turnern und Sportlern ist ein ähnliches traditionell freundliches Deutschenbild anzutreffen.
Etwas pointiert formuliert läßt sich feststellen, daß bei jedem Sit-in an einer Universität, bei jeder Vernissage progressiver Kunst, bei jeder avantgardistischen Redaktion in aller Welt, eine große Chance besteht, daß die Akteure eher deutschfeindlich sind, daß dagegen bei der Errichtung einer Militärregierung oder bei einem Turn-, Sport- oder Schützenfest die Teilnehmer wahrscheinlich zur Deutschenfreundlichkeit tendieren.
Eine weitverbreitete Ideologie haben übrigens unsere Untersuchungen nicht bestätigt. Die jungen Leute im Ausland unterscheiden sich durchwegs in ihrer Deutschfreundlichkeit kaum von den älteren. Die Ansicht der Aufklärer von der Jugend ohne Vorurteile ist eine Illusion. Das Lebensalter spielt als Faktor bei der Bildung bestimmter nationaler Stereotype eine untergeordnete Rolle.

Erwin Rommel (1891−1944), deutscher Feldmarschall im 2. Weltkrieg
Carl von Clausewitz (1780−1831), preußischer General und Militärtheoretiker
Friedrich Hölderlin (1770−1843), deutscher Lyriker

Task 1:
Listen and follow the text. Find out how the text is constructed by giving the numbers of the lines where you can find the following points.

Lines

_____ a An account of a personal experience

_____ b A summary of the chapter *Bilder bei soziographischen Gruppen*

_____ c A common characteristic of officers throughout the world

_____ d Comments on an illusion about young people

_____ e A conclusion from a personal experience

Eine große Gruppe oft nicht gerade wenig einflußreicher Herren tendiert dagegen dazu, deutschfreundlich zu reagieren: Die Militärs der ganzen Welt. Sowohl ein Feldwebel der amerikanischen Marine, wie ein Offizier indischer Gurkha-Truppen, wie der Anführer einer südamerikanischen Militärjunta wird vermutlich einen gewissen Hang zur Deutschenfreundlichkeit haben. Ein Erlebnis aus Nepal mag die Gründe für die Deutschenfreundlichkeit der Militärs demonstrieren.

nicht gerade	− *not exactly*
der Feldwebel	− *sergeant*
der Anführer	− *leader*
vermutlich	− *presumably*
der Hang zu	− *tendency towards*
das Erlebnis	− *experience*

Task 2:
Read lines 3−10 once again. Look up further words in the *Basic Word List* where necessary. Then answer the questions.

a What are *die Militärs der ganzen Welt* described as?
b What common characteristic is shared by the corporal, officer and Junta-leader?
c What is an experience on the part of the author intended to demonstrate?

Der Militärattaché an der indischen Botschaft in Kathmandu gehörte einem Gurkha-Regiment an. Er ist sehr erfreut, einen Deutschen zu sehen. Er büffelt gerade, um eine Prüfung zu bestehen, die er braucht, um in den indischen Generalstab aufgenommen zu werden. Hierzu liest er die Schriften deutscher Militärtheoretiker, teilweise im Originaltext. Im Augenblick studiert er die Schlachten Rommels in Nordafrika.

(line 15)

die Botschaft	– embassy
büffeln	– to swot up
hierzu	– for this
im Augenblick	– at the moment
die Schlacht	– battle

Task 3:
Find the German equivalents in the text and write them down.

a *he is very pleased*

_____

b *in order to pass an examination which he needs*

_____

Task 4:
Read lines 11–18 once again. Look up further words in the *Basic Word List* where necessary. Then answer the questions.

a What does the text say about the Indian's career to date?
b What are his plans for the future?
c Which hurdle will he first have to negotiate?
d How is he preparing himself for this task?
e What is he reading at the moment?

Er lädt mich am nächsten Tag zum Tee ein und holt ein Buch hervor, das er wie eine Bibel heilig hält. Es ist Clausewitzens Schrift „Vom Kriege" in einer billigen Volksausgabe. Er reicht mir den Band und ich muß ihm die deutschen Sätze langsam vorsprechen, so wie bei einer Dichterlesung. Verzückt sitzt der junge indische Offizier und hört, wie ich ihm die deutschen Sätze langsam vorlese, als seien es Gedichte von Hölderlin.

(lines 20, 25)

einladen	– to invite
hervorholen	– to bring out
heilig	– holy, sacred
reichen	– to pass, to hand
verzückt	– enraptured
vorlesen	– to read (aloud)
die Dichterlesung:	reading of a poet or writer from his own works

Task 5:
Find the German equivalents in the text and underline them.

a *the next day*
b *Clausewitz's work in a cheap popular edition*
c *I have to slowly read the German sentences aloud to him*
d *as if they were poems by Hölderlin*

Task 6:
Read lines 18–25 once again. Look up further words in the *Basic Word List* where necessary. Then describe in detail what happens the next day over tea.

Ein Offizier, der sich Clausewitz wie ein Gedicht vortragen läßt, kann kein Feind der Deutschen sein. Auch bei Turnern und Sportlern ist ein ähnliches traditionell freundliches Deutschenbild anzutreffen.

sich etwas vortragen lassen	– to have something recited to one
der Feind	– enemy
der Turner	– gymnast
der Sportler	– sportsman
ist anzutreffen	– can be found

Task 7:
Read lines 26–29 once again. Look up further words in the *Basic Word List* where necessary. Then answer the questions.

a What conclusion does the author draw from the meeting?
b In how far can gymnasts and sportsmen be compared with the officer?

Etwas pointiert formuliert läßt sich feststellen, daß bei jedem Sit-in an einer Universität, bei jeder Vernissage progressiver Kunst, bei jeder avantgardistischen Redaktion in aller Welt, eine große Chance besteht, daß die Akteure eher deutschfeindlich sind, daß dagegen bei der Errichtung einer Militärregierung oder bei einem Turn-, Sport- oder Schützenfest die Teilnehmer wahrscheinlich zur Deutschenfreundlichkeit tendieren.

(lines 30, 35)

die Vernissage	– opening day (of an art exhibition)
bestehen	– to exist
der Akteur, -e	– protagonist
das Turnfest	– gymnastics festival
der Schütze	– rifleman
das Schützenfest:	a fair featuring shooting matches

Task 8:
Find the German equivalents in the text and underline them.

a *to put it rather pointedly*
b *in every avant-garde editorial office*
c *during the establishment of a military government*
d *that . . . the participants probably tend to be amicably disposed towards the Germans*

Task 9:
Read lines 30–37 once again. Look up further words where necessary. Then answer the questions.

a Where or when can one probably encounter people hostile to Germans?
b Where or when can one probably encounter people who are amicably disposed towards Germans?

> 40 Eine weitverbreitete Ideologie haben übrigens unsere Untersuchungen nicht bestätigt. Die jungen Leute im Ausland unterscheiden sich durchwegs in ihrer Deutschfreundlichkeit kaum von den älteren. Die Ansicht der Aufklärer von der Jugend ohne Vorurteile ist eine Illusion. Das Lebensalter spielt als Faktor bei der Bildung bestimmter nationaler Stereotype eine untergeordnete Rolle.

übrigens	– by the way
sich unterscheiden	– to differ
durchwegs	– in every way, without exception
die Ansicht	– opinion, view
aufklären	– to enlighten
der Aufklärer	– here: propagandist
bestimmt	– certain

Task 10:
Find the German equivalents in the text and write them down.

a *our investigations have not confirmed . . .*

_____

b *the young people abroad*

_____

c *youth without prejudices*

_____

d *age is of secondary importance*

_____

Task 11:
Read lines 38–44 once again; then answer the questions.

a Which widely-held opinion was clearly refuted by the study?
b What is the real state of affairs?

Task 12:
Read the whole text through once again. Then give your opinion on the following questions.

a In how far, in your experience, is the author's account true?
b What interest could a government have in having the image of the nation abroad investigated?
c What might have been the reaction of the government which commissioned this investigation to these results?

Grammar

1 *hier*-Compounds
(Cf. *Hier-compounds*, p. 42).

Die Intelligenz ist nicht deutschfreundlich. Der Grund *hierfür (for this)* liegt im reaktionären Image der Deutschen.

Er büffelt gerade, um eine Prüfung zu bestehen . . . *Hierzu (for this purpose)* liest er die Schriften deutscher Militärtheoretiker.

2 *als* + subjunctive in comparisons
(Cf. *Comparisons with „als ob"*, p. 98f.)

Verzückt sitzt der indische Offizier und hört, wie ich ihm die deutschen Sätze langsam vorlese, *als seien es (as if they were)* Gedichte von Hölderlin.

3 Two uses of *lassen*
(Cf. *Verbs: „lassen"*, p. 77)

a Ein Offizier, der sich Clausewitz wie ein Gedicht *vortragen läßt,*
An officer who has *Clausewitz* recited *to him like a poem . . .*

b Etwas pointiert formuliert *läßt sich feststellen,* daß . . .
To put it rather pointedly, it may be observed *that . . .*

4 Verb *sein* + infinitive with *zu*
(Cf. *Verbs: „sein", III*, p. 74)

Auch bei Sportlern *ist* ein ähnliches Deutschenbild *anzutreffen*.
In the case of sportsmen, too, one can encounter *a similar image of Germans.*

Manchmal *ist* ein unmittelbarer Einfluß kommunistischer Propaganda *zu spüren*.
Sometimes a direct influence of communist propaganda can be noticed.

5 Two uses of *bestehen*

a Er büffelt gerade, um eine Prüfung zu bestehen *(to pass an exam)*
b . . . , daß eine große Chance besteht *(exists, there is)*

Word formation

1 Prefix *hervor-*
(Cf. *Prefixes,* p. 128)

hervorholen	– *to bring out*	(holen	– *to fetch, to bring)*
hervorheben	– *to emphasize*	(heben	– *to lift, to raise)*

2 Prefix *ein-*
(Cf. *Prefixes,* p. 126)

eintreten	– *to step in; to occur*	(treten	– *to tread, to step)*
einladen	– *to invite*	(laden	– *to load)*
einschließen	– *to include; to surround*	(schließen	– *to shut, to close, to conclude)*
eingeschlossen	– *included*		
Einfluß	– *influence*	(Fluß	– *flow, stream)*
Einkommen	– *income*	(kommen	– *to come)*
Einführung	– *introduction*	(führen	– *to lead)*

3 Nouns derived from irregular verbs
Derivatives from irregular verbs such as *sehen, gehen, schreiben, kommen* often look somewhat different.

die Ansicht *opinion, view*	from: ansehen *to look at, to regard*	die Schrift *writing*	from: schreiben *to write*
der Rückgang *decrease, drop*	zurückgehen *to go back*	die Übereinkunft *agreement, understanding*	übereinkommen *to agree*
der Vorgang *process*	vorgehen *to proceed*		

Deutsche Fragen

Texte zur jüngsten Vergangenheit

Ein Lese- und Arbeitsbuch für den Deutschunterricht

von K.-H. Drochner
unter Mitarbeit von Erika Drochner-Kirchberg

KURT TUCHOLSKY – THOMAS MANN – ADOLF HITLER – KURT VON SCHROEDER – WALTER SCHÖNSTEDT – GOTTFRIED BENN – BERTOLT BRECHT – ALEXANDER UND MARGARETE MITSCHERLICH – AXEL EGGEBRECHT – WALTER KEMPOWSKI – THEODOR W. ADORNO – SEBASTIAN HAFFNER – ERICH KÄSTNER – HANS MAYER – ALFRED SCHÜTZE – GOLO MANN – JEAN AMÉRY – KURT GERSTEIN – KARL JASPERS – KLAUS MANN – HERMANN KESTEN – ZE'EV SCHUL – PETER WEISS – ALFRED DÖBLIN – INGE DEUTSCHKRON – DIE WEISSE ROSE – MAX VON DER GRÜN – FIETE SCHULZE – HEINZ KÜPPER – GÜNTER GRASS – HORST KRÜGER – ALFRED KANTOROWICZ – RICHARD MATTHIAS MÜLLER – HEINRICH BÖLL – HANS MAGNUS ENZENSBERGER – KURT SONTHEIMER – WILHELM BLEEK – MANFRED KOCH-HILLEBRECHT – MARLIES MENGE – ROLF SCHNEIDER – WILHELM RÖPKE – KONRAD ADENAUER – WOLFGANG SEIFFERT – KLAUS HARPPRECHT – MARTIN WALSER – JOHANNES GROSS – GERHARD ZWERENZ – HANS CHRISTOPH BUCH

Einführungen in den zeitgeschichtlichen Zusammenhang, Fragen zum Textverständnis, zum Inhalt und zur Sprache erschließen die Texte, die Anlaß zur Diskussion bieten und einen lebendigen Deutschunterricht ermöglichen.
207 Seiten. Bestellnummer 49460

Langenscheidt